THE ARAB CONQUESTS
IN
CENTRAL ASIA

BY

H. A. R. GIBB

AMS PRESS
NEW YORK

Reprinted from the edition of 1923, New York
First AMS EDITION published 1970
Manufactured in the United States of America

Library of Congress Catalog Card Number: 75-111477
SBN: 404-02718-0

AMS PRESS, INC.
New York, N.Y. 10003

CONTENTS

v

PREFACE

THE first draft of this work was presented to the University of London in December 1921, under the title of "The Arab Conquest of Transoxania", as a thesis for the degree of Master of Arts, and was approved by the Senate in January 1922, for publication as such. During the year my attention was taken up in other directions and, except for the publication of two studies on the subject in the Bulletin of the School of Oriental Studies, nothing further was done until by the generosity of the Trustees of the Forlong Bequest Fund an opportunity of publication was offered. In its present form the work has been largely rewritten and revised. It makes no claim to present a complete historical account of the Arabs in Central Asia, but is intended solely as a critical study of the authorities in greater detail than has hitherto been made. Much is therefore omitted because it has already been dealt with in the standard histories. In order to keep down the cost of publication, the extensive references which originally accompanied the text have been cut down to a few notes at the end of each chapter. No references are given when, as in the great majority of cases, the authority for the statements made can easily be found in the appropriate place either in Tabarī or Balādhurī.

I regret that several works which are indispensable for a thorough study of the subject have, for linguistic reasons, been inaccessible to me. Such are van Vloten's *Opkomst der Abbasiden*, and almost the whole range of Russian research work. Through the kindness of Sir Denison Ross, however, I have been able to avail myself of a draft MS. translation of the most important and valuable of them all, Professor W. Barthold's

Turkestan, as well as of his as yet unpublished London lectures on " The Nomads of Central Asia." My sincere thanks are due to Sir Denison Ross also for his continued interest and material assistance ever since he first introduced me to the subject ; to Sir Thomas Arnold for much encouragement and helpful counsel ; to Professor Barthold, who has read the MS. through and made a number of valuable suggestions ; to the Trustees of the Forlong Bequest Fund for their kindness in undertaking the publication ; and in no small measure to my wife, who has given much time and labour to preparing the MS. for publication.

London,
    April, 1923.

I. INTRODUCTION

Early History.

The Oxus is a boundary of tradition rather than of history. Lying midway between the old frontier of Aryan civilisation formed by the Jaxartes and the Pamir and the natural strategic frontier offered by the north-eastern escarpment of the plateau of Īrān, it has never proved a barrier to imperial armies from either side. It was not on the Oxus but on the Jaxartes that Alexander's strategic insight fixed the position of Alexander Eschate, and when the outposts of Persian dominion were thrust back by the constant pressure of the Central Asian hordes, their retreat was stayed not on the Oxus but on the Murghāb. Thus when the tide of conquest turned and the Arabs won back her ancient heritage for Persia, they, like Alexander, were compelled to carry their arms ever further to the East and all un-knowing re-establish the frontiers of the Achaemenid Empire. It was from the legends of Sāsānian times, enshrined in the pages of the historians and the national epic of Firdawsī, that the Oxus came to be regarded as the boundary between Īrān and Tūrān.

Through all the centuries of invasion, however, the peoples of Sogdiana and the Oxus basin remained Iranian at bottom, preserving an Iranian speech and Iranian institutions. But the political conditions of the country at the period of the Arab conquests were so complex that it is necessary to trace briefly the course of their development.

The second century B.C. was a period of upheaval in Central Asia : the powerful Hiung-Nu peoples were dispossessing weaker tribes of their pasture lands and forcing them to migrate westwards. Between 150 and

B

125 B.C. a succession of nomadic tribes, the last and most powerful of which were a branch of the Yueh-Chi, were driven down into Sogdiana. It is now generally held that these tribes were of Aryan origin, though the question is not perhaps settled with absolute certainty. Before long, however, a second group, the K'ang, possessed themselves of Sogdiana, driving the Yueh Chi on into Bactria and the Afghan mountains (1). In these districts they found, alongside the Iranian peasantry, a settled population of Tukhari (in Chinese, Ta-Hia), already noted in the Chinese annals for their commercial enterprise (2), and while at first the nomad tribes introduced complete confusion, it would seem that they rapidly absorbed, or were absorbed by, the native elements, and thus assimilated the Hellenistic civilisation of Bactria. From this fusion arose, about 50 A.D., the powerful Kushan Empire which spread into India on the one side and probably maintained some form of suzerainty over the K'ang kindgoms of Sogdiana on the other. Under the new empire, Buddhism was acclimatised in Turkestan, and Sogdiana developed into a great *entrepôt* for Chinese trade with the West. Towards the close of the third century the Kushan Empire, weakened by attacks from the new national dynasties in India and Persia, reverted to its primitive form of small independent principalities, which, however, retained sufficient cohesion to prevent a Persian reconquest. It is practically certain that Sāsānian authority never extended beyond Balkh and rarely as far. In the fourth and fifth centuries references are made to a fresh horde of nomads in the north-east, the Juan-Juan (Chionitae, Avars) (3), but it does not appear that any new settlements were made in the Oxus countries.

In the middle of the fifth century, another people, the Ephthalites (Arabic Hay*t*al, Chinese Ye-Tha), perhaps a branch of the Hiung-nu, not only completely overran the former Kushan territories, but by successive defeats of the Persian armies forced the Sāsānid Kings to pay tribute. The Ephthalites appear to have been a nomadic people organised as a military caste of the familiar Turkish type, and the existing institutions and principalities, in large part at least, continued side by side with them (4). Their rule was too transitory to produce any lasting effects, or to inflict any serious injury on the commerce and prosperity of Sogdiana.

The rise of the Central Asian empire of the Turks proper (Tu-Kueh) dates from their overthrow of the Juan-Juan in Mongolia in 552, under their great Khan, Mokan. His brother Istämi (the Silzibul of the Byzantine historians), the semi-independent jabghu of the ten tribes of Western Turks, after consolidating his power in the Ili and Chu valleys, formed an alliance with Khusrū Anūshīrwān, and in a joint attack between 563 and 568 the two powers completely overthrew the Ephthalite kingdom and divided their territories. For a brief moment the Oxus was the actual boundary between Īrān and Tūrān ; under pressure from the silk traders of Sogdiana, however, the alliance was broken and the weaker successors of Anūshīrwān could scarcely do more than maintain their outpost garrisons on the Murghāb. From this time the Ephthalites, like the Kushans, were gradually assimilating to the Iranian population (5), though the change was less rapid in the Cisoxine lands of Lower Tukhāristān, Bādghīs, and Herāt, where Ephthalite principalities were re-constituted, probably with Turkish support, and continued to give Persia much trouble on her north-eastern frontiers (6). On the other hand the Turks of the five western tribes (Nu-she-pi), who became independent after the break up of the Great Khanate about 582, maintained their suzerainty over Sogdiana and the middle Oxus basin by frequent expeditions, in one case at least as far as Balkh. There is no trace in our records of extensive Turkish immigration into the conquered lands ; at most, small groups of Turks wandered south with their herds, especially, it would seem, south of the Iron Gate (7). In general, Turkish

interference in the administration of the subject principalities was at first limited to the appointment of military
governors and the collection of tribute. Thus, in the
semi-legendary account given by An-Naysābūrī of the
Turkish conquest of Bukhārā the Bukhār Khudāh is
represented as the chief dihqān under the Turkish
governor. It is possible also that the native princes
maintained guards of Turkish mercenaries.

At this period, therefore, so far from the Oxus
being a barrier, there was considerable intercommunica-
tion between the peoples on either side, and at least the
elements of a racial and cultural unity, in spite of political
divisions. This is a factor of importance in the history
of the Arab conquests : the conquest of Transoxania is
intimately linked with the fortunes of Lower Tukhāristān, and only became possible when the latter country
was completely subdued. On the other hand, the
Jaxartes formed a natural racial and political frontier.
" Shāsh and Sughd have seldom run together " says
Vambery, and in spite of nominal annexations on more
than one occasion Muslim rule was not effectively
imposed on Shāsh and Farghāna until some time after
the final conquest of Transoxania. Their chief importance for the history of Transoxania is that they
formed the jumping-off place for counter-invasions
from the East. It is not without significance that of the
two battles which were decisive in establishing Arab rule
in Sogdiana one was fought to the west of Balkh and the
other on the Talas river, far into the Turkish lands
beyond the Jaxartes (see pp. 84 and 96).

Political Divisions.

Researches into Chinese records have now made it
possible to obtain a more definite idea of the political
conditions of these frontier provinces in the seventh
century. All the principalities acknowledged the Khan
of the Western Turks as overlord and paid tribute to
him under compulsion, though, as will appear, there is

good cause for doubting whether a Turkish army ever
came in response to their appeals for support until the
rise of the Türgesh power in 716.

Geographically the cultivated lands to the west and
south-west of the middle Jaxartes are divided by the
Hissar mountains into two well-defined areas. The
northern area includes the rich valley of the Zarafshān
and the lesser streams which descend the northern slope
of the watershed, the southern comprises the broad
basin formed by the Oxus and its tributaries between
the mountains of the Pamīr and the steppelands. The
former, which as a whole is called Sogdiana in distinction from the smaller principality of Sughd, was at
this period divided between a number of small states,
each independent of the others but forming together a
loose confederacy in a manner strikingly reminiscent of
the Hellenic city-states. The strongest bond of union
was formed by their mutual interest in the Chinese silk
trade, the chief stations of which were at Samarqand,
Paykand, and Kish. The premier city was Samarqand,
the pre-eminence of which and high culture of whose
population is vouched for by Yuan-Chwang. Special
emphasis is laid on their enterprise and success in trade,
and a number of early embassies, doubtless commercial
missions, are recorded from Samarqand and Bukhārā
to the Chinese court. The merchant families of Paykand, according to Tomaschek's rendering of Narshakhī
(8), were Kushans, but Iranian elements, reinforced by
emigrants from the Sāsānid dominions, formed the
majority in the cities. The agricultural population was
almost if not entirely Iranian.

A second link between the majority of the cities was
formed by the ruling house of the Shao-wu, if, as the
Chinese records assert, these all belonged to one royal
family. The head of the clan governed Samarqand and
was allied by marriage to the Turkish Khan ; cadet
branches ruled in Ushrūsana, Kish, Bukhārā, and the
lesser principalities in the basin of the Zarafshān. In

the later lists the rulers of Shāsh and Farghāna as well as
the Khwārizm Shāh are shown as belonging to the clan
also, though with less probability (**9**). Whether the
family were of K'ang origin, or, as the Chinese records
state, belonged to the Yueh-Chi, they appear in the
Arabic histories with Persian territorial titles (Khudāh,
Shāh, and the general term dihqān). Some of the princes
also possessed Turkish titles, probably conferred on them
as vassals of the Khan. The ruler of Samarqand, as
king of Sughd, is called the Ikhshīdh or Ikhshēdh, which
is easily recognised as the Persian *khshayathiya*. This
title was borne also, as is well known, by the king of
Farghāna. It is certain at least from both Chinese and
Arabic accounts that these rulers were not Turks. The
Turkish names by which they are sometimes called were
given out of deference or compliment to their Turkish
suzerains, just as Arabic names begin to appear amongst
them immediately after the Arab conquests. Particularly misleading is the name Tarkhūn which appears
more than once in the list of princes of Samarqand and
has been erroneously taken as the title Tarkhān, though
it is in reality only the Arabic transcription of a personal
name spelt in the Chinese records Tu-hoen. During
the six or seven hundred years of their rule all these
princes had become fully identified with their Iranian
subjects (**10**). The " kingship " moreover was not a
real monarchy but rather the primacy in an oligarchical
system. Their authority was far from absolute, and the
landed aristocracy (dihqāns) and rich merchants possessed, as will be seen later, not only a large measure of
independence but also on occasion the power to depose
the ruling prince and elect his successor. As the
succession appears to have been largely hereditary it is
probable that, according to Iranian custom, eligibility
was confined to a single royal house. In some cases,
it would seem, the succession was regulated during the
lifetime of the reigning prince by some such method as
association in the principate, probably combined with

the appointment of the remaining princes to other fiefs (**11**).

The "confederacy" of these states, however, was in no sense an alliance and probably amounted to little more than a *modus vivendi*. Besides the more important princes there existed an enormous number of petty autocrats, some possibly Turkish, others probably descended from former conquerors, whose authority may sometimes have scarcely extended beyond the limits of their own villages. In lands subject to the Turks and patrolled by nomadic tribes an effective centralised government was hardly possible. Mutual antagonisms and wars cannot have been uncommon though we have now no record of them, except that during the early Arab period there was hostility between Bukhārā and Wardāna, but the latter cannot be reckoned among the Shao-wu principalities since, according to Narshakhī, it was founded by a Sāsānid prince about 300 A.D. Until the profitable Chinese trade was threatened by the Arabs we find no trustworthy record of combined resistance offered by the country to its piecemeal reduction, and only long after the conquests of Qutayba is there any hint of a concerted rising. At the same time, the strength of the cities and warlike nature of their inhabitants may be gauged from the way in which they not only preserved themselves from destruction at the hands of their successive nomad invaders, but even gained their respect, while this, in some respects perhaps the most highly civilised of all the lands subdued by the Arabs (**12**), proved also the most difficult to conquer, and most intractable to hold.

The same lack of unity is apparent in the districts south of the Iron Gate, though nominally subject to a single authority. It is important to bear in mind that the Zarafshān and Oxus valleys were completely independent of one another—that the difference between them was not merely one of government, but also of language, and even, to some extent, of blood, owing to the greater mixture of races in the southern basin. When, occasionally, as in the "Mūsā legend", reference is made in the Arabic histories to common action by Sughd and Tukhāristān, it is due to a complete misunderstanding of the state of the country prior to the conquest, and it is worthy of notice that no such reference is to be found in any narrative otherwise reliable. On his outward journey in 630, Yuan Chwang found the country divided into twenty-seven petty states under separate rulers, with the chief military authority vested in the Turkish Shād, the eldest son of the Jabghu of the Western Turks, who had his seat near the modern Qunduz. During the period of anarchy which befell the Western Turks in the following years, the whole district was formed into an independent kingdom under a son of the former Shād, who founded the dynasty of Jabghus of Tukhāristān. Minor Turkish chiefs and intendants probably seized similar authority in their own districts, and though the Jabghu was recognised as suzerain of all the lands from the Iron Gate to Zābulistān and Kapisa and from Herāt to Khuttal (13), his authority was little more than nominal except within his immediate district of Upper Tukhāristān. The lesser princes, in Shūmān, Khuttal, &c., many of whom were Turkish, appear to have acted quite independently and did not hesitate to defy their Suzerain on occasion. The name Tukhāristān is used very loosely in the Arabic records, with misleading effect (14). How relatively unimportant to the Arabs Tukhāristān proper was is shown by the fact that its annexation (see below p. 38) is passed over in silence. The brunt of the resistance offered to the early Arab conquests was borne by the princes of Lower Tukhār-istān, i.e., the riverain districts south of the Iron Gate, including Chaghāniān and Balkh, together with the Ephthalite principalities in Jūzjān, Bādghīs, and Herāt, and possibly the mountainous fringe of Gharjistān. This explains why the Arabs always regarded Balkh, the old religious capital of the Kushan Empire and site of the famous Buddhist shrine of Nawbahār, as the capital of the " Turks " ; it was in fact the centre of what we might almost term the " amphictyony " of Lower Tukhāristān, combining strategic and commercial importance with religious veneration. Long after the Nawbahār had been destroyed by Ibn 'Āmir this sentiment continued to exist in the country (15).

A chance narrative in Tabarī (II. 1224 f.), which, though of Bāhilite origin, can scarcely have been invented, indicates the situation in Lower Tukhāristān in 710. In the presence of Qutayba, the Shād and as-Sabal (King of Khuttal) do homage to the Jabghu, the former excusing himself on the ground that though he has joined Qutayba against the Jabghu, yet he is the Jabghu's vassal. The Ephthalite prince of Bādghīs then does homage to the Shād, who must consequently be regarded as the chief prince in Lower Tukhāristān. His indentification with the Jabghu himself in another passage (Tab. II. 1206. 9) is obviously impossible. Though certainty on the point is hardly to be expected, the description best suits the king of Chaghānian (Chāghān Khudāh), who consistently adopted an attitude of cooperation with the Arabs. It would seem too that the king of Chaghānian commanded the armies of Lower Tukhāristān in 652 and again in 737. Moreover, an embassy to China on behalf of Tukhāristān in 719 was actually despatched by the king of Chaghānian, which implies that he held a status in the kingdom consonant with the high title of Shād. The conclusion drawn by Marquart and Chavannes that the king of Chaghānian and the Jabghu were identical is disproved by the Chinese records (16).

Such conditions of political disunion were naturally all in favour of the Arabs. It might have seemed also that the general insecurity, together with the burden of maintaining armies and courts and the ever-recurring ravages of invasion, would move the mass of the population to welcome the prospect of a strong and united

government, more especially as so large a proportion of
the Muslim armies were composed of their Persian kin.
For the Arabic records in general are misleading on two
important points. By their use of the word " Turk "
for all the non-Persian peoples of the East, they give the
impression (due perhaps to the circumstances of the time
in which the chief histories were composed) that the
opponents of the Arabs in Transoxania were the historical
Turks. The truth is that until 720 the Arab invaders
were resisted only by the local princes with armies
composed almost entirely of Iranians, except perhaps
on one or two special occasions when Turkish forces may
have intervened. The other error is in interpreting the
conquests as primarily wars for the Faith. Rebellion,
for instance, is expressed in terms of apostasy. It is now
well established that this conception is exaggerated ;
religious questions did not, in fact, enter until much
later and even then chiefly as expressions of political
relationships. To the Iranian peasantry, themselves
steadfastly attached to the national cults, the advent of
another faith in this meeting-place of all the cultures
and religions of Asia at first carried little significance.
Two factors in particular combined to provoke a resistance so stubborn that it took the Arabs a century
merely to reduce the country to sullen submission. The
first of these was the proud national spirit of the
Iranians which was eventually to break down the
supremacy of the Arabs and give birth to the first
Persian dynasties in Islām. The few wise governors of
Khurāsān found in this their strongest support, but,
outraged again and again by an arrogant and rapacious
administration, the subject peoples became embittered
and sought all means of escape from its tyranny. The
second was the interest of the commercial relations on
which the wealth and prosperity of the country depended. This again might have disposed the cities to
accept a rule which promised not only stability, but a
wide extension of opportunity. The Arab governors,

as we shall see, were not indeed blind to this, but the exactions of the treasury, and still more the greed of local officials, combined with the unsettlement of constant invasion to create an attitude of distrust, which deepened later into despair. It must not be forgotten that the commercial ties of the Sogdians were much stronger with the East than with the West, and that this too prompted them to cultivate relations with the Turks and Chinese rather than with the Arabs when the necessity of making a choice was forced upon them.

The Arabic Sources.

The early Arabic sources are remarkably rich in material for the reconstruction of the conquests in Khurāsān and Transoxania. For the earlier period the narratives of Ya'qūbī and Balādhurī are nearly as full as those of Tabarī, but the special value of the latter lies in his method of compilation which renders the traditions amenable to critical study and thus provides a control for all the others. Moreover, while the other historians, regarding the conquests of Qutayba as definitely completing the reduction of Transoxania, provide only meagre notices for the later period, Tabarī more than compensates for their silence by the enormous wealth of detail embodied in the accounts he quotes from Al-Madā'inī and others of the last thirty years of Umayyad rule. As a general rule, these three historians rely on different authorities, though all use the earlier histories of Al-Madā'inī and Abū 'Ubayda to some extent. The monograph of Narshakhī (d. 959 A.D.) based on both Arabic and local sources, with some resemblance to Balādhurī, is unfortunately preserved only in a Persian version of two centuries later which has obviously been edited, to what extent is unknown, but which probably represents the original as unsatisfactorily as Bal'amī's Persian version of Tabarī. Even so it preserves to us some account of the peoples against whom the Arab invaders were matched, and thus does a little to remedy the defects of the other historians in this respect. It may well be doubted, however, whether some of its narratives merit the reliance placed upon them by van Vloten (17). The much later historian Ibn al-Athīr introduces very little new material, but confines himself for the most part to abridging and re-editing the narratives in *T*abarī, with a tendency to follow the more exaggerated accounts. The geographer Ibn Khūrdādhbih gives a list of titles and names, which is, however, too confused to supply any reliable evidence.

Reference has already been made to certain aspects of the conquests in which the Arab historians are misleading. Their information on the Turks and the principalities of Sogdiana can now, fortunately, be supplemented and parts of their narratives controlled from Chinese sources, chiefly through Chavannes' valuable " Documents sur les Tou-Kiue (Turcs) Occidentaux." But there are two other facts which also demand attention : one, that the Arabic authorities, as we possess them, and even with all allowance made for their limitations, are by no means exhaustive ; *i.e.*, reliance on omissions in the narratives is an unsafe principle of criticism : the other, that by critical study it is possible to distinguish at certain points several lines of tendentious tradition or legend, directed to the interests of national feeling or of some particular tribe or faction, and centred in some cases round specific persons. These may most conveniently be summarised as follows :

1. A Qaysite tradition, centred on the family of Ibn Khāzim :
2. An Azd-Rabī'a tradition, centred on Muhallab and hostile to *H*ajjāj. This became the most popular tradition among the Arabs, and is followed by Balādhurī, but opposed by Ya'qūbī :
3. A Bāhilite tradition, centred on the tribal hero, Qutayba b. Muslim. In general it found little favour but is occasionally quoted somewhat sarcastically by *T*abarī.

4. A local Bukhārā tradition, followed by Ya'qūbī, Balādhurī and Narshakhī. It presents the early conquests under the form of an historical romance, centred on the Queen Khātūn in the part of a national Boadicea. Other local traditions, which are frequently utilised by Ṭabarī, seem to be much more free from serious exaggeration :

5. The few notices in Dīnawarī follow an entirely divergent and extremely garbled tradition from unknown sources, which may for the most part be neglected :

6. The quotations made by Balādhurī (e.g. 422. 10) from Abū 'Ubayda show the influence of a re-writing of episodes with an anti-Arab bias, directed to the interests of the Shu'ūbīya movement, in which Abū 'Ubayda was a prominent figure (**18**).

7. In the later period, there appears also the fragments of a tradition of which Naṣr b. Sayyār is the hero.

Some, if not all, of these traditions developed in some detail, and where they are not balanced by other versions they present a distorted narrative of events, verging in some cases on the fictitious. The most noteworthy examples of this are the Khātūn legend (see below p. 18) and the typical story of the exploits of Mūsā b. Khāzim in Transoxania in a style not unworthy of Bedouin romance (**19**). It is therefore most important to disentangle these variant traditions and assign its proper value to each. The Bāhilite accounts of Qutayba's conquests, for instance, contain wild exaggerations of fact, which, nevertheless, have sometimes been utilised in all seriousness by modern historians, amonst other purposes to establish synchronisms with the Turkish inscriptions (**20**).

With these precautions, it is possible to follow up and reconstruct, with comparative certainty and completeness, that progress of the Arab arms in Central Asia whose vicissitudes are outlined in the following pages.

NOTES
(Full Titles in Bibliography)

1. Franke, Beiträge 41 ff., 67. Cordier, Chine I, 225.
2. If Marquart's identification (Ērānshahr, 201f.) is correct.
3. Cordier I. 229 : Ērānshahr 50 ff.
4. Yuan Chwang I. 103. Prof. Barthold suggests that the connection between the Ephthalites and the Huns may have been political only, not racial.
5. Chavannes, Documents 155 : Ērānshahr 89.
6. *Tab.* I. 2885. 13 and 2886. 3 : Ya'qūbī, History, II, 193 : Yāqūt (ed. Wüstenfeld) I. 492 : Balādhurī 403 : Ērānshahr 65 f., 77 f., and 150. Bādghīs was still a nomad pasture-ground in the XIVth century : Ibn. Baṭṭūṭa, II, 67 f.
7. Yuan Chwang I. 105 ; II. 266 ; Chav. Doc. 161 : Ēranshahr 250 ff.
8. Tomaschek, Soghdiana, 170.
9. See Marquart, Chronologie, 71 : Shiratori in Keleti Szemle III (1902) foot-note to pp. 122–3.
10. Cf. Narshakhī 29. 4. On the Iranisation of nomadic elements, Blochet, Introduction a l'Histoire des Mongols, (Leyden, 1910) p. 211 note ; Peisker, The Asiatic Background, pp. 353–6.
11. Chavannes, Notes 91, and cf. below p. 80.
12. *Cf.* Barthold, in Zeitschrift fur Assyriologie XXVI (1911) p. 262.
13. Yuan Chwang I, 75 n. 2, 102 ff : II 270 : Chav. Doc. 200 f.
14. *E.g.* Tab. II, 1448, 7–10 : *cf.* Ērānshahr 228.
15. *Cf.* Ya'qūbī, Geog. 287 : Tab. II 1205. 12 : Ērānshahr 66, 87 ff.
16. Chavannes, Doc. 201, Notes 37.
17. Narshakhī's unreliability is even more marked in his account of the origins of the Sāmānid dynasty : *cf.* Barthold, Turkestan 215 n. 3.
18. See Goldziher, Muhammadanische Studien, I, 195 ff.
19. Prof. Barthold has drawn my attention to the fact that the story of Mūsā also includes (twice over) an episode from the popular legend of Zopyrus. See his article in Zapiski XVII (1906) 0141, and Wellhausen, Arabische Reich, 257, 265.
20. *E.g.* Marquart, Chronologie, p. 8.

II. THE EARLY RAIDS

The Conquest of Lower Tukhāristān.

Arab legend relates that the Muslim forces, pursuing Yazdigird from the field of Nihāwand in 21/642, had already come in contact with the " Turks " of Tukhāristān before the death of 'Omar. But the final destruction of the Sāsānid power and first imposition of Arab rule on Khurāsān only followed ten years later, by the troops of 'Abdullah ibn 'Āmir, 'Othmān's governor in Basra. The Ephthalites of Herāt and Bādghīs submitted without a blow, and the first serious check to their advance was met in the Murghāb valley, when al-Aḥnaf b. Qays with an army of 4,000 Arabs and 1,000 Persians found himself opposed by the organised forces of Lower Tukhāristān and was compelled to retire on Merv-Rūdh. A second expedition under al-Aqra' b. Ḥābis, however, defeated a weaker force in Jūzjān, and subsequently occupied Jūzjān, Fāryāb, Tālaqān, and Balkh. Small divisions made plundering raids into the neighbouring territories, *e.g.*, to Siminjān (a town within the frontiers of Tukhāristān proper, governed by a Turkish prince, the Ru'b Khān), and to Khwārizm, not always with success ; on the other hand, a successful raid was made on Māyamurgh in Sogdiana in 33/654, which is mentioned by Abū 'Ubayda alone of the Arabic authorities (1). A general insurrection which broke out shortly afterwards, headed by a certain Qārin, apparently a member of the noble Persian family bearing that name, seems to have been instrumental in causing the Arabs to evacuate Khurāsān for a time (2), though several raids are recorded of 'Alī's governors between 35 and 38 A.H. These earliest " conquests," in fact, were little more than plundering raids on a large scale, the effect of that movement of expansion whose momentum was carrying forward the Arabs irresistibly. According to the Chinese records, which, however, require to be used with caution at this point, the retreat of the Arabs in 655 was followed up by the army of *T*ukhāristān who reinstated Pērōz, the son of Yazdigird, as titular king of Persia (**3**).

When peace was restored to Islām by the recognition of Mu'āwiya in 41/661, Ibn 'Āmir was again entrusted with the conquest of Khurāsān. The same rough and ready methods were adopted as before ; there appears to have been no definite plan of invasion, and even the order of governors is uncertain. Not only are traditions relating to A.H. 32 and 42 confused by the different authorities, but a vast amount of the whole is affected by tribal legends. Hints of fierce resistance are given from time to time. Qays b. al-Haytham, the governor's first legate, was faced with a fresh revolt in Bādghīs, Herāt, and Balkh. He recaptured the latter and in retaliation destroyed the famous shrine of Nawbahār, but left the Ephthalites to be dealt with by his successor, 'Abdullah ibn Khāzim. It is clear that there was no ordered progress of the Arab arms until Khurāsān was brought under the administration of Ziyād b. Abīhi. After an experimental division of the province under tribal leaders, a policy obviously dangerous and quickly abandoned, Ziyād, realising the danger of allowing Persian nationalism a free hand in the East, backed up by the resources of *T*ukhāristān, centralised the administration at Merv, and organised a preventive campaign. In 47/667 his lieutenant, al-*H*akam b. 'Amr al-Ghifārī, opened a series of campaigns directed to the conquest of Lower *T*ukhāristān and Gharjistān, in the course of which he crossed the Oxus and carried his arms into Chaghāniān, and drove Pērōz back to China in discomfiture. On his death, three years later, the conquered provinces rose in revolt, but the new governor, Rabī' b. Ziyād al-*H*ārithī, the first conqueror of Sijistān, after reducing Balkh, pursued the Ephthalite army into Quhistān and dispersed it with great slaughter. Again an expedition was sent across the Oxus into Chaghāniān (clearly indicating the connection between Chaghāniān and Lower Tukhāristān), while another directed down the left bank of the river secured Zamm and Āmul, the two chief ferry points for Sogdiana. Mention is also made of a conquest of Khwārizm. All these expeditions seem to point to a methodical plan of conquest, arranged between Ziyād and his governors ; the Arab power was thus firmly established, for the moment at least, in the Cisoxanian lands, and the way prepared for the invasion of Sogdiana. A further important step was the colonisation of Khurāsān by fifty thousand families from Baṣra and Kūfa (4), settled according to Arab practice in five garrison towns, for the double purpose of securing the conquests already made, and providing the forces for their further extension.

The First Invasion of Bukhārā and Sughd.

Although at this junction Ziyād himself died, his policy was carried on by his sons, in particular by 'Ubaydullāh. Scarcely any governor, not even Hajjāj, has suffered so much at the hands of the traditionists as the " Murderer of Husayn," though his ability and devotion to the Umayyads are beyond question. It is not surprising therefore that his earlier military successes should be so briefly related, in spite of their importance. Yet as he was no more than 25 years of age when appointed by Mu'āwiya to the province of Khurāsān on probation, and only two years later was selected to fill his father's position in 'Irāq, his administration must have been markedly successful. The policy of Ziyād had now firmly secured Khurāsān and made it feasible to use it as a base for the extension of the conquests into the rich lands across the river. On his arrival at Merv, therefore, in the autumn of 53/673, the new governor began preparations for an invasion of Bukhārā.

The Shao-wu principality of Bukhārā was at this time second in importance only to Samarqand. It included

c

not only the greater part of the oasis (" al-Bukhārīya ")
then much more thickly populated than now, but also the
great emporium of Paykand, which controlled the trade
route across the Oxus at Āmul.   Of its early history we
have two accounts, both confused, inaccurate in detail,
and often conflicting.   From these it may be gathered
that the prince, who held the high Turkish title of Shad
(5), resided at Paykand, the citadel of Būkhārā being either
founded or restored by the Bukhār Khudāh Bidūn, probably
in consequence of the Arab invasions.   This prince at his
death left a son only a few months old on whose behalf
the regency was exercised by the Queen-Mother.   This
princess, known under the title of Khātūn (a Turkish
form of the Sogdian word for " lady ") became the central
figure in the local traditions, which represent the Arab
invasions as occurring precisely during the period of her
regency.   This version is the one accepted by Balādhurī,
Ya'qūbī, and Narshakhī, but though not altogether
devoid of historical value, it is certainly misplaced, and
the true account of the early conquests must, for cogent
reasons, be sought in the brief and widely divergent
narratives of Tabarī.   In the first place the Khātūn-
legend, like all such legends, has grown by natural
elaboration of detail, as in the account given by Narshakhī
of Khātūn's administration of justice and by continual
accretions from other streams of tradition, as seen, on
comparing the narratives of Balādhurī and Narshakhī,
in the introduction of episodes of Ibn Khāzim and Muhallab.   Critical examination also reveals alternative
traditions and chronological inconsistencies, as, for
example, the birth of Tughshāda after the invasion of
Sa'īd b. 'Othmān, Khātūn's reign of 15 years, and others
mentioned below.   There is clear evidence of the late
compilation of the tradition in the frequent references to
" Tarkhūn, king of Sughd," though his reign did not begin
until considerably after 696 (6).   It may be noticed that
in the variant account of the conquests prefixed to the
Persian edition of Narshakhī and ascribed to An-

Naysābūrī there is no reference at all to Khātūn. Moreover there are indications that Tabarī was aware of the local tradition and completely rejected it ; this, at least, would account for the unusual practice of specifying Qabaj-Khātūn as " the wife of the king " in 54 A.H. Even Balādhurī rejects the more fantastic developments of the legend. Tabarī's narratives, however, require to be collated with the additional material in Balādhurī, who has not relied entirely on the local tradition. The germ of the native version is probably to be found in a confusion of the Arab conquests with the later war between Bukhārā and Wardāna (7), whose echoes are heard in Qutayba's invasions thirty years after.

In the spring of 54/674 'Ubaydullah b. Ziyād crossed the river and marched directly on Paykand. After a partial success, he led his forces forward towards Bukhārā and severely defeated the army of the Bukhār Khudāh. From Tabarī's narrative, which relates only that two thousand men of Bukhārā, skilful archers, were taken by 'Ubaydullah to Basra, where they formed his personal guard, it is left to be inferred that a treaty was concluded under which the Bukhār Khudāh became tributary. The local tradition magnifies the expedition by adding a siege of Bukhārā (during the winter) and bringing in an army of Turks to assist Khātūn, but confirms the success of the Arabs. 'Ubaydullah's practice on this occasion of forming a bodyguard or retinue of captives appears to have been a common one. 'Abdur-Raḥmān ibn Samura had previously brought captives from Sijistān to Basra, where they built him a mosque, and later governors of Khurāsān continued the practice, as will be seen. In this may be recognised perhaps the germ of the Turkish guards recruited by the later 'Abbāsid Caliphs.

'Ubaydullah's successor, Aslam b. Zur'a, remained inactive, but in 56/676 Sa'īd b. 'Othmān, who had obtained the governorship of Khurāsān by importuning Mu'āwiya, carried the Arab arms more deeply into Transoxania, defeated the Sughdians in the open field and reduced their city.   Taking fifty young nobles as hostages, he retired from Sughd and subsequently occupied Tirmidh, an important fortress on the Oxus controlling the main North and South trade route, having presumably marched through the Iron Gate.   The conquest of Sughd was thus definitely co-ordinated with that of Chaghāniān.   Tabarī's narrative is strangely vague and abrupt ; it contains no mention of Bukhārā nor any definite reference to Samarqand, except for the statement that it was the objective of Sa'īd's expedition.   Using this narrative alone, one would be inclined to suspect that the city captured by Sa'īd was not Samarqand but Kish (since it has been established by Marquart that Kish was formerly called Sughd), and that the reference to Samarqand was due to a later misunderstanding of the name (8).   On the other hand, both the local tradition and Abū 'Ubayda speak of a siege of Samarqand by Sa'īd, though their narratives are far from being in agreement in detail, and there are other indications of confusion between Sa'īd and Salm b. Ziyād.   All accounts except Narshakhī's, however, agree that the hostages who were carried by Sa'īd to Madīna and there murdered him were Sughdians (9).   Baladhurī's tradition of Sa'īd's expedition is as follows.   On his crossing the river, Khātūn at first renewed her allegiance, only to withdraw it again on the approach of an army of Turks, Sughdians, and men of Kish and Nasaf, 120,000 strong.   Sa'īd, however, completely defeated the enemy and after a triumphal entry into Bukhārā, marched on Samarqand, his forces swelled by Khātūn's army, besieged it for three days and made it tributary.   On his return he captured Tirmidh and while there received the tribute due from Khātūn and the allegiance of Khuttal.   Narshakhī's account is the same in essentials, adding only a number of imaginative details.

Sa'īd was unable to retain his position in Khurāsān, and for five years the conquests were stayed (except for summer raids) under the indolent Aslam b. Zur'a and the

avaricious 'Abdur-Raḥmān b. Ziyād. In 61/680–681
Yazīd I appointed Salm, another son of Ziyād, to
Khurāsān and Sijistān. Eager to emulate his brother,
Salm, even before leaving Baṣra, announced his intention
of renewing the expeditions into Transoxania and enlisted
a picked force on the spot, including such tried leaders as
Muhallab b. Abī Sufra and 'Abdullah b. Khāzim. From a
poem preserved in the Ḥamāsa of Abū Tammām (10)
it would appear that somewhat unwilling levies for this
expedition were raised even in Mesopotamia. Towards
the close of the winter a surprise attack was made on
Khwārizm, with some success. Ṭabarī gives two versions
of this expedition, the first of which is a highly embroi-
dered one from the Muhallabite tradition. During the
same year, Salm marched into Sughd and occupied
Samarqand, where he appears to have made his headquarters over the winter. Balādhurī mentions a sub-
sidiary raid on Khujanda under A'shā Hamdān, in which,
however, the Muslims were defeated, and a Sughdian
revolt which was crushed with the loss of its leader, here
called Bandūn. The name is almost certainly to be read
as that of the Bukhār-Khudāh, Bīdūn (11), and in view
of the silence of Ṭabarī raises rather a difficult problem.
It may be conjectured that what Balādhurī intended was
a revolt of the Bukhariots, combined with Sughdian
forces. The origin of this statement may perhaps be
sought for in the Bukhārā tradition, which Balādhurī
does not follow in his general account of the expeditions
of Salm, but which he may have tried to work in with the
other. On the other hand he nowhere refers to Bīdūn
as the Bukhār Khudāh. As related by Narshakhī and
Ya'qūbī Salm's expedition is directed solely against
Bukhārā. Khātūn, on promising her hand to Ṭarkhūn,
receives a reinforcement of 120,000 men from Sughd, and
Bīdūn (here still alive) recruits an army in " Turkistān,"
including the " Prince of Khotan." After severe fighting,
the Muslim forces, numbering 6,000, kill Bīdūn and rout
the unbelievers, taking so much booty that the share of

each horseman amounts to 2,400 dirhems. Khātūn, thoroughly humbled by this decisive proof of Arab invincibility, sues for peace and pays a heavy tribute. Beyond the fantastic exaggerations and incoherencies of the legend, there is nothing inherently improbable in a Bukhariot revolt. In support of this view, it may be remarked that the death of Bīdūn at this point would agree with the slender data we have for the internal wars which probably formed the original basis of the Khātūn-legend, and would also provide a foothold for the later developments of the tradition. Without fuller evidence, however, we can get no further than reasonable conjecture.

After the conquests made by Salm, which probably occupied the years 682 and 683, it seemed as though the Arabs were on the verge of imposing their rule on Transoxania when civil war broke out in the heart of the Empire. Even allowing for the fact that these expeditions were little more than raids, the comparative ease with which the Arabs held to ransom the richest cities in the country is astonishing. The explanation can lie only in their mutual exclusiveness. There is not a hint of united action in the field in Tabarī's accounts (12). A factor which may have exercised some influence was that Sogdiana was completely isolated during these years and unable to look for support from without. The power of the Western Turks was broken by the Chinese armies between 645 and 658 ; Chinese forces are said to have reached as far west as Kish, and the Emperor Kao-Tsung had officially annexed all the territories formerly included in the Turkish dominions. In the latter year the provinces of Sogdiana and the Jaxartes were organized in sixteen districts, including a " Government of Persia " under the Pērōz already mentioned, situated apparently in Sijistān, possibly even in Eastern Khurāsān (13). The immediate practical effect of this change of status was of little moment, but her nominal annexation gave China a prestige which was destined to exercise immense influence in determining the attitude of the peoples of Sogdiana to the Arabs. From 670 to 692, however, the new power of Tibet held the Chinese armies in check in the Tarim basin and cut off all possibility of Chinese intervention in the West. The Sogdian princes were thus thrown on their own resources, and, ignorant as yet of the danger behind the Arab raids, they seem to have bowed to the storm. It must not be forgotten that the cities had never before met such an enemy as the Arabs. They had been accustomed to plundering raids by Turks, who disappeared as quickly as they came, and who, disliking to undertake a lengthy siege, were easily appeased by a ransom. Familiar with such nominal annexations, they would naturally adopt the same tactics against the new invaders. Had the Arabs maintained their pressure, there was thus every prospect that Transoxania would have been colonised with a tithe of the expense and loss incurred in its reconquest and would have become as integral a part of the Muslim dominions as Khurāsān. But the opportunity was lost in the fratricidal struggles of the factions, and when the Arabs recommenced their encroachments, the determined resistance offered to their advance showed that the lessons of the first invasion had not been lost on the native princes.

The Withdrawal of the Arabs.

The tribal feuds which occupied the Arabs of Khurāsān left the princes of Transoxania free to regain their independence. It would seem even that Lower Tukhāristān was not only in part lost to the Arabs but that local forces took the offensive and raided Khurāsān. On the gradual restoration of order under Umayya, however, Lower Tukhāristān again recognised, at least in name, the Arab suzerainty (14). Meanwhile, a strange episode had occurred in Chaghānian. Mūsā, the son of 'Abdullah ibn Khāzim, sent by his father to secure a safe place of retreat, had captured the strong fortress of Tirmidh,

from which he continually raided the neighbouring
districts. His exploits were worked up in popular story
into an epic of adventure, in which legend has almost
overlaid historical fact. The most fantastic exaggerations were devised in order to provide a suitable background for the incredible deeds of valour indulged in
by the hero. But in truth his actual exploits were
sufficiently amazing, and all the efforts of the forces of
the local rulers (magnified in the legend to huge armies of
" Turks and Hay*t*al and Tibetans ") although aided
on one occasion by a force of Khuzā'ites, were unable to
dislodge him. For fifteen years he remained in secure
possession of his stronghold, a refuge for the disaffected
from all sides, and a standing example of the helplessness
of the rulers across the river.

In 77/696 Umayya re-opened the campaigns into
Transoxania. An expedition to Khwārizm was successful
(**15**), another across the Oxus narrowly escaped destruction. Balādhurī mentions, with doubtful accuracy, a
successful raid on Khuttal, which may, however, only be a
variant on this. An expedition directed against Bukhārā,
which is said to have had Tirmidh as a second objective,
was hurriedly abandoned on the fresh outbreak of revolt
under Bukayr b. Wishā*h* in Khurāsān. Though the
revolt failed in its immediate object, a most serious
situation had been created. Bukayr had endeavoured
to rally the Persians to his side by promising all converts
remission of Kharāj. The opportunity was undoubtedly
seized by large numbers, and the pacification occasioned
some negotiations between Umayya and Thābit b. Qu*t*ba,
an influential noble who acted as spokesman for the
mawālī of Eastern Khurāsān. Umayya's reimposition of
Kharāj, however, caused widespread unrest (**16**) and made
prompt action necessary. 'Abdul-Malik at once recalled
his hapless kinsman (in 78) and made Khurāsān a depen-
dency of 'Irāq under the government of *H*ajjāj. This
far-sighted governor had already dealt with a desperate
situation of the same sort in 'Irāq and reduced it to

outward tranquillity. The same extreme measures that had been adopted there were not necessary in Khurāsān; its troubles were due less to insurgent mawālī than to the factions of Qays. Hajjāj was himself a strong Qaysite, but he was not the man to put party before the interests of the State. The first necessity was to appoint a governor who could be trusted to repress both forms of anarchy and in Muhallab such a man was available. His tribe of Azd was not yet strong enough in Khurāsān to cause the risk of opening a new channel for factional strife, and his military reputation fitted him for carrying out Hajjāj's policy of active campaigning as an antidote to internal dissension. It is possible that Hajjāj had in mind from the first a definite conquest of Transoxania, but for a few years nothing more than sporadic raids took place.

Muhallab's first care, however, was to encourage the settlement of Azd in Khurāsān, until he was supported by a division equal in size to any other. After securing the crossing at Zamm in 80/699 he marched into the district of Kish and there established his headquarters for two years, besieging the city and sending out minor expeditions under his sons in various directions (17). Yazīd was sent with a force into Khuttal, nominally to co-operate with a pretender to the throne, but met with little success ; Habīb, sent against Rabinjān, found himself countered by the forces of Bukhārā. Balādhurī's account of Muhallab's campaigns is ludicrously exaggerated ; Tabarī quotes Muhallab himself as discouraging any attempts at effecting a conquest. On the death of his son al-Mughīra in Rajab 82, he came to terms with Kish and abandoned his expeditions, but died in the following Dhu'l-Hijja (Jan. 702) near Merv Rūdh, and was succeeded by his son Yazīd.

The Muhallabite tradition which represents the appointment as distasteful to Hajjāj but popular in Khurāsān is almost certainly influenced by the later hostility between Yazīd and Hajjāj. It is probable,

however, that *H*ajjāj, whose policy was to keep his
governors dependent on himself, viewed with suspicion
the concentration of authority in the hands of the leader
of a powerful hostile clan, but he was content to wait for
the meantime and give Yazīd sufficient rope to hang himself. Except for an attempted raid on Khwārizm
Yazīd carried out no expeditions, while under his government the precarious internal balance of Khurāsān was
soon upset. The quarrels of Qays had been composed by
Muhallab, but they were in no mood to bear with the
leadership of the parvenu Azd ; already before the
death of Muhallab, in spite of the Tamīmite eulogy
quoted by *T*abarī, there was a moment when the feud
threatened to break out. The pronounced factional
leanings of Yazīd strained the situation still further.
Even more serious was the attitude of the mawālī.
*H*urayth, the brother of Thābit ibn Qu*t*ba, had been left
behind at Kish by Muhallab to collect the tribute, but on
his return was scourged for disobedience. The disgrace
cut *H*urayth deeply ; too late Muhallab realised the
gravity of his act, but *H*urayth spurned his overtures
and with Thābit fled to Mūsā at Tirmidh. Yazīd retalia-
ted with foolish severity by maltreating their families,
which only inflamed the general resentment. *H*urayth
and Thābit used their influence to stir up an insurrection
to act in concert with Mūsā ; the king of Chaghānian
and his Ephthalite confederates headed by Nēzak, prince
of Bādghīs, readily responded, while Persian interest was
excited by the return to *T*ukhāristān of the son of Pērōz,
the heir of the Sāsānids. It seems probable that even some
of Qays were a party to the scheme (**18**). Seizing an
opportunity when Yazīd was occupied with the rebel
forces of Ibn al-Ashath on the borders of Khurāsān the
revolt broke out. Yazīd was powerless to prevent the
expulsion of his residents from Chaghānian and Lower
*T*ukhāristān, and Mūsā is said to have refrained from
invading Khurāsān only from fear that it would fall into
the hands of Thābit and *H*urayth. Even the success

claimed for Yazīd in Bādghīs can have been of little effect (**19**). Fortunately for the Arabs, Mūsā's jealousy of Thābit and *H*urayth caused a division in the ranks of their enemies, but though the brothers both fell in battle, the danger remained acute. The son of Pērōz still lingered in *T*ukhāristān, and even at Damascus there was some uneasiness about the situation in Khurāsān (**20**).

To *H*ajjaj it was obvious that the first essential was to reunite the Arabs and that so long as Yazīd was in power that was impossible. The only difficulty was to find a governor acceptable to Qays and to substitute him without risking a revolt of Azd. It was solved with admirable ingenuity. By ordering Yazīd to transfer his authority to his weaker brother Mufa*dd*al, *H*ajjāj at one stroke removed the man from whom he had most to fear and prevented him from uniting Azd in opposition, although Yazīd realised that the fall of his house was imminent. At the same time the Caliph's permission was sought for the nomination of Qutayba ibn Muslim as governor of Khurāsān. Belonging to the neutral tribe of Bāhila, Qutayba was reckoned as allied to Qays, but might be trusted to hold the scales evenly between the factions ; he had already distinguished himself in 'Irāq and in his governorship of Rayy, and was the more devoted to *H*ajjāj in that he was protected by no strong party of his own. The accepted belief that *H*ajjāj took no steps to remove the family of Muhallab until Mūsā was put out of the way is based on a remark attributed to Muhallab in the Mūsā-legend, which is frequently contradicted elsewhere both expressly and by implication.

Mufa*dd*al, during his nine months of office in 85/704, seems to have endeavoured to impress *H*ajjāj by a show of military activity against the rebels in Bādghīs. At the same time, acting in concert with the local princes (magnified in the legend to " *T*arkhūn and as-Sabal "), he sent an expedition to Tirmidh under 'Othmān b. Mas'ūd. Mūsā was cut off and killed in a sortie and his nephew Sulaymān surrendered at discretion. *H*ajjāj's first exclamation on hearing the news is said to have been one of anger at the insult to Qays, but the last hindrance to the appointment of the new governor was now removed and towards the close of the year Qutayba b. Muslim arrived in Merv.

NOTES

1. Bal. 408. 5 : Chav., Doc. 172, n. 1. There were two localities called Māya-murgh in Sughd : one near Samarqand (Istakhrī 321. 6), and the other one day's march from Nasaf on the Bukhārā road (ibid. 337. 7). According to the Chinese records the former is the one in question here.
2. Yāqūt, ed. Wüstenfeld, II. 411. 21 : cf. Caetani, " Annali " VIII. 4 ff. On Qārin, Nöldeke, Sâsaniden 127, 437 : Marquart, Ērānshahr 134.
3. Chav., Doc. 172.
4. Cf. Lammens, " Ziād b. Abīhi " (R.S.O. 1912) p. 664.
5. Cf. with Tughshāda the name of the reigning prince in 658, Chav., Doc. 137.
6. Chav., Doc. 136.
7. Narshakhī 8 and 30.
8. Chronologie 57 : Ērānshahr 303 f. This view is supported also by the letter from the king of Samarqand to the Emperor of China in 718 (see p. 60), which puts the first Arab conquest some 35 years before, i.e. in 682 or 683.
9. Accounts also in Kitāb al-Aghānī I. 18 : Ibn Qutayba 101.
10. Hamāsa, ed. Freytag, I. 363-4.
11. Cf. Barthold, " Turkestan " 103 n.1.
12. The account given in Tab. II. 394 of the annual meeting of the " Kings of Khurāsān " near Khwārizm for mutual counsel not only possesses little intrinsic probability, but is obviously intended to magnify the exploits of Muhallab. In this case, fortunately, the authorities quoted by Tab. leave no doubt as to the Azdite origin of the narrative. Madā'inī's version is given ib. ll. 19 sq.
13. Wieger, Textes Historiques, 1608 f : Chav., Doc. 273 ff : Marquart, Ēran, 68.
14. Tab. II. 490, 860 ff. : Bal. 414 f. : I. Athīr, IV. 66 : Anon. (ed. Ahlwardt), 195.
15. Abū 'Ubayda ap. Bal. 426. 10 : cf. Lestrange, " Lands of the Eastern Caliphate " p. 448, note.
16. Tab. 1031 : cf. Anon. 310 f.
17. Tab. 1040 f., 1078. 5 : Ya'qūbī, Hist. II. 330.
18. Cf. Tab. 1152 with 1185. 5.   For the son of Pērōz, Chav., Doc. 172.
19. Cf. Tab. 1129 with 1144 and 1184.
20. Anon. 337.

III. THE CONQUESTS OF QUTAYBA

THE achievements of the Muslim armies in Central Asia during the reign of Walīd I were due in the first place to the complete co-operation between the directive genius of Hajjāj and the military capacity of Qutayba. Qutayba's strategic abilities have been somewhat overrated, though the Arabic texts are at no pains to conceal the fact that his gifts fell something short of genius. On more than one occasion we are shown in what constant touch the viceroy was kept with the progress of his armies, and how large a part he took in drawing up the plan of campaign, though the credit of carrying it through to a successful issue rightly belongs to Qutayba. Hajjāj seems to have had the fullest confidence in his lieutenant, and if he did not hesitate to utter reproof and warning when occasion required, he.was equally quick to express appreciation of Qutayba's success. The Arabs of all parties soon realised that behind their general lay the authority of Hajjāj, the wholesome respect inspired by whom prevented any open breach during his lifetime. The second factor which materially assisted the conquests was that in their prosecution Qutayba united all parties in Khurāsān, Persians and Arabs, Qays and Yemen. It was no small matter to keep their enthusiasm unabated in the face of campaigns so protracted and severe, nor can the enthusiasm be explained only by the attraction of a rich booty. It is by no means improbable that Qutayba's success was really due more to his talent for administration than to his generalship. He seems to have realised, as no other Arab governor in the east had yet done, that in such a province as Khurāsān the safety and security of the Arab government must depend in the long run on the co-operation of the Persian populace, who formed so great a majority in the country. The bitterness of factional

strife had shown how unsafe it was to rely on the support
of the Arabs alone, especially in the face of such a movement as Yazīd had provoked.   By his conciliatory
attitude, therefore, Qutayba earned the confidence of the
Persians and repaid it with confidence ; from his constant
employment of Persian agents and his growing prefer-
ence for Persian governors, it would seem even that he
came to regard them as forming the " 'Ashīra " he lacked
among the Arabs.   Although it earned him the ill-will
of the Arabs and played a great part in his fall, it may be
that in this he was instrumental in giving the first impulse
to the recovery of a national sentiment amongst the
Persians of Khurāsān.

The situation in Central Asia was also favourable for
a renewal of the attempt to annex to the Arab dominions
the rich lands of Transoxania, though it is doubtful how
much information the Arabs possessed on this point.
In 682, while China, weakened internally by the intrigues
of the Empress Wu, had her hands tied by the wars with
Tibet, the Eastern or Northern Turks had re-asserted
their independence.   The new Empire never regained
its authority over all the western territories of the former
Khans, but by constant campaigns had extended its rule
over the Ten Tribes of the Ili and Chu, who, we are
told, were " almost annihilated."   In 701 the Eastern
Turks invaded Sogdiana, but there is no reason to assume,
though it has frequently been suggested, that Muhallab's
forces at Kish were affected by this raid.   As the necessity
of securing hostages for the safety even of the lines of
communication shows, the hostility of the local forces is
sufficient to explain all the encounters narrated.   The
devastation and loss that invariably accompanied these
raids must have still further weakened the resources of
the subject princes, to whom there was small consolation
in the appointment of a son of the Khan to command the
Ten Tribes.   In any case the unceasing warfare which
the Eastern Turks had to wage against the Türgesh
from 699 to 711 effectually prevented them from sending

assistance in response to any appeals for support which may have reached them from Sogdiana (1). Equally if not more impossible was it for the Türgesh to intervene in Sogdiana during the same period (2). By the " Turks," as we have seen, the Arab historians mean as a general rule the local inhabitants, amongst whom there may quite possibly have been included at that time Turkish elements. Occasional references to the Khāqān (unless they may be taken to refer to local chiefs, which is improbable) are obvious *fakhr*-developments. The narrative of 98 A.H. on which the theory of Türgesh intervention is mainly based, is a pure Bāhilite invention. Finally, the experience of the Arabs in later years shows us that, if the resistance of Sogdiana had been backed by large forces of Turks, it would have been impossible for Qutayba to achieve so large a measure of success.

The conquests of Qutayba fall naturally into four periods :

1. 86/705 : The recovery of Lower *T*ukhāristān ;
2. From 87/706 to 90/709 : The conquest of Bukhārā ;
3. From 91/710 to 93/712 : Consolidation of the Arab authority in the Oxus valley and its extension into *S*ughd ;
4. From 94/713 to 96/715 : Expeditions into the Jaxartes provinces.

The recovery of Lower Tukhāristān.

The first task before Qutayba was to crush the revolt of Lower *T*ukhāristān. In the spring of 86/705 the army was assembled and marched through Merv Rūdh and *T*ālaqān on Balkh. According to one of *T*abarī's narratives the city was surrendered without a blow. A second account, which, though not explicitly given as Bāhilite, may be regarded as such, since it centres on Qutayba's brother and is intended to establish a Bāhilite claim on the Barmakids, speaks of a revolt amongst some of the inhabitants. This may perhaps be the more correct version, since we hear of Balkh being in a ruinous condition four years later (*T*ab. 1206. 1). The submission of Balkh was followed by that of Tīsh, king of Chaghāniān, who had probably cooperated with Mufa*dd*al in the attack on Tirmidh the year before. His action was, it seems, inspired by a feud with the king of Shūmān and Ākharūn, in the upper valleys of the Surkhan and Penjab rivers, against whom he hoped to use the Arab troops in return for his assistance to them. Mufa*dd*al had actually projected an expedition against Shūmān before his recall, and it was now carried out by Qutayba, who was perhaps the more ready to undertake it since it assured the safety of the southern approach to the Iron Gate. After the submission of the King Ghīslashtān, who was of Turkish blood, according to Yuan-Chwang, Qutayba returned to Merv alone, leaving the army to follow under his brother Sāli*h*, who carried out a number of minor raids on the way. It is obvious that, in spite of Balādhurī's imaginative account, these raids must be located in the districts neighbouring on the Oxus. The readings in *T*abarī's narrative are, however, defective (**3**). Having thus isolated Nēzak in Bādghīs, the heart of the revolt, Qutayba spent the winter months in negotiating with him through Sulaym " the Counsellor," an influential Persian whose skill in conducting the most difficult negotiations proved more than once of the utmost value to Qutayba. Nēzak was persuaded to surrender and was conducted to Merv, where peace was concluded on condition that Qutayba would not enter Bādghīs in person. As a precautionary measure however the governor arranged that Nēzak should accompany him in all his expeditions. Thus for the moment at least, the danger of an outbreak in Khurāsān was averted, in a manner honourable to both parties, and the son of Pērōz took his way back to China to await a more favourable opportunity (**4**).

The Conquest of Bukhārā.

In the following year, Qutayba, first making sure of the crossings at Āmul and Zamm, opened his campaigns in Bukhārā with an attack on Paykand. From the expressions of Narshakhī, on whose history of this period we may place more reliance since his details as a rule fit in with and supplement the other histories, it can be gathered that the principality of Bukhārā was weakened by civil war and invasion. During the minority of Tughshāda and the regency of Khātūn, the ambitious nobles had struggled between themselves for the chief power ; most of the territories, including Bukhārā itself, had been seized by the prince of Wardāna and the remaining districts seem to have been brought under the rule of Khunuk Khudāh, a noble who assumed the title of Bukhār Khudāh (5). Paykand was thus more or less isolated and, from Narshakhī's account, seems to have been left to its fate. The battle with the Sughdians related in Tabarī is an obvious anticipation from the events of the following year. After a siege of some two months the city came to terms with Qutabya, who left it under a small garrison and, according to Tabarī's version, began the return march to Merv. An émeute in Paykand, however, brought him back at once. It seems reasonable to assume that the citizens, imagining Qutayba's attack to have been no more than an isolated raid, tried to expel the garrison as soon as he retired. The details given in Narshakhī, that on Qutayba's advance towards Bukhārā a certain citizen, enraged by the insulting conduct of the governor, Warqā' b. Naṣr al-Bāhili, attempted to murder him, are trivial and unconvincing. Whatever the cause of the revolt may have been, however, Qutayba took a terrible revenge. In accordance with mediaeval practice the renegade city was sacked, its fighting men put to death, and its women and children enslaved. The booty taken from this, the first of the great trading cities of Central Asia to be forcibly captured by the Arabs, furnished inexhaustible

D

material for the exaggerated details of later tradition. The most important part of the spoil was an arsenal of weapons and armour, the excellence of which was such that the " forging of Sughd " appears in contemporary verse alongside the traditional " forging of David " for superlative craftsmanship (6). With the consent of Hajjāj, these weapons were not included in the division of the booty but used to re-equip the army. The statement that there were only 350 suits of armour in the whole army before this is, however, of Bāhilite provenance and scarcely worthy of credence. The exemplary punishment thus meted out by Qutayba to Paykand at the beginning of his career was a stern warning to Nēzak and the Sogdians. Those who accepted Arab dominion would be humanely treated, but any attempt at rebellion would be inexorably crushed. Nevertheless the sentence on Paykand was somewhat mitigated in the sequel, as Narshakhī adds that the captives were ransomed by the merchants of Paykand on their return from the annual trading expedition to China, and the city, after lying in ruins for many years, was eventually rebuilt.

The disaster at Paykand roused the princes and merchants of Transoxania to the danger of neglecting the invaders. The feud between Wardāna and Bukhārā was patched up ; round Wardān Khudāh, the central figure and organiser of the struggle for independence, gathered the forces of all the nearer principalities. Thus when Qutayba, on renewing his expedition in 88/707, had taken the outlying town of Tūmushkath (not Nūmushkath, which was the earlier name of Bukhārā) and Rāmīthana (or Rāmtīn), he found his communications cut by the troops of Wardāna, Bukhārā, and Sughd. It is not, perhaps, impossible that the prince of Farghāna should have cooperated with the Sughdians, as stated in Madā'inī's account. On the other hand the Arabic narratives are far from explicit, and the Sughdians here referred to are much more probably those of Kish than of Samarqand, a suspicion which is confirmed by the

famous punning order of *H*ajjāj : " Crush Kish, destroy
Nasaf, and drive Wardān back." Narshakhī and Ya‘-
qūbī gives an account of the negotiations between
*H*ayyān an-Naba*n*ī, representing Qutayba, and *T*arkhūn
king of *S*ughd, which is certainly to be put, with *T*abarī,
after the conquest of Bukhārā two years later. Throughout all these campaigns there is manifest a tendency,
common to the early chronicles of all nations, to exagger-
ate the numbers and composition of the opposing forces.
As usual the Bāhilite account carries this to the point of
absurdity by introducing a *T*ürgesh force of no less than
200,000 men, an obvious anachronism, influenced by the
later Türgesh invasions. The connection is made clear
by the mention of Kūr Maghānūn, whom we find nearly
thirty years later (*T*ab. II. 1602. 2) as " one of the chiefs
of the Türgesh." The true account would seem to be
that Qutayba did not attempt to fight a pitched battle,
but by dilatory tactics wearied out the allies and gave
time for their natural inclination towards disunion to
operate, then evaded them by a rapid march through the
Iron Gate and, except for a rearguard skirmish with the
enemy's cavalry, got his army clear across the river at
Tirmidh. The appointment of ‘Abdur-Ra*h*mān ibn
Muslim to command the rearguard gives us the clue, as
it was to this brother that Qutayba regularly entrusted
all the most difficult commands. In the following year
Qutayba was still unable to make headway against the
united forces of Wardān Khudāh, Kish and Nasaf, and
after protracted fighting (in spite of the double victory
claimed by the Bāhilites) returned to Merv. For this
weakness he was severely reprimanded by *H*ajjāj, who,
with the aid of a map, drew up a plan of attack. The
invasion of 90/709 seems to have taken Wardān Khudāh
by surprise, as the Muslim army was able to advance at
once to the siege of Bukhārā. There is some ground for
the conjecture, however, that the death of Wardān
Khudāh had occurred in the interval and that Qutayba
was opposed only by the local forces (**7**). This may also

explain the hesitation of the forces of Samarqand to intervene. The battle before the walls of Bukhārā is described by Tabarī in a long Tamīmite tradition reminiscent
of the ancient " days," but the actual capture of the city
is left to be inferred. This siege is transferred to
Wardāna by Vambery (*cf. Heart of Asia* p. 52)
probably on the authority of the Persian Tabarī (Zotenberg IV. 165), but Narshakhī, Tabarī and all other
authorities quite definitely refer to Bukhārā. Abū
'Ubayda's tradition (Bal. 420) of capture by treachery is
at best a confusion with the capture of Samarqand. All
the details given in Narshakhī relative to Qutayba's
organisation of Bukhārā do not refer to this year ; most
probably the only immediate measures taken were the
imposition of a tribute of 200,000 dirhems and the occupation of the citadel by an Arab garrison.

A diplomatic success followed the victory at Bukhārā.
Tarkhūn, king of Samarqand, opened negotiations with
Qutayba, who was represented by the commander of his
Persian corps, Hayyān an-Nabañ, and terms were agreed
upon, probably on the basis of the old treaty made by
Salm ibn Ziyād. Tarkhūn gave hostages for the payment
of tribute and Qutayba began the march back to Merv.

Consolidation and Advance.

If the Arabs returned in the autumn of 90/709 elated
with their success, they were soon given fresh cause for
anxiety. Nēzak, finally realising that all hope of recover-
ing independence must be extinguished if Arab rule was
strengthened in Khurāsān, and perhaps putting down to
weakness Qutayba's willingness to gain his ends if possible
by diplomacy, determined on a last effort to overthrow
Muslim sovereignty in Lower Tukhāristān, at the moment
when it was least to be expected. Having obtained
permission to revisit his home, he left Qutayba at Āmul
and made for Balkh, but escaped to Tukhāristān in order
to avoid re-arrest. From here he corresponded with the
rulers of Balkh, Merv Rūdh, Tālaqān, Fāryāb, and Jūz-

jān, urging them to undertake a concerted rising in the spring. The king of Chaghānīān seems to have refused to countenance the conspiracy, but the weak Jabghu of Tukhāristān was induced, possibly by force, to make common cause with Nēzak, who hoped doubtless by this means to unite all the subject princes in defence of their suzerain.

Qutayba's army was already disbanded and the winter was setting in. All that he could do was to despatch the garrison at Merv, some 12,000 men, under 'Abdur-Raḥmān, with instructions to winter in Balkh, where they could counter any immediate move by Nēzak, and advance into Tukhāristān in the spring. This resolute action made Qutayba master of the situation and so intimidated the rebels that when, in the early spring, the Arabs marched through the disaffected districts, scarcely a blow was struck and the princes either submitted or fled. The inhabitants were granted a complete amnesty except at Talāqān, concerning which the traditions are hopelessly confused. According to one account, a band of robbers were there executed and crucified, but it is possible that it was selected for special severity because there alone the revolt had openly broken out (**8**). There was probably also some reorganization of the administration of Lower Tukhāristān, in the direction of conferring fuller powers on the Arab governors installed in each district, though the native princes continued to exercise a nominal authority. From Balkh, Qutayba marched forward and rejoined 'Abdur-Raḥmān. With the assistance of the lesser princes they pursued and captured Nēzak, who was subsequently executed on direct orders from Ḥajjāj, in violation of Qutayba's promise of pardon (**9**). How little this action was condemned by the prevailing spirit of the age, however, is shown by the contemporary poems quoted by Tabarī, lauding the " defender of the precincts of Islam " and comparing his action to the measures formerly adopted against the Jewish tribes of Madīna. Yet even at this time we find traces of the new spirit that was to make itself more felt in later years, and hear voices raised, like Thābit Qu*t*na's, against the " treachery that calls itself resolution." *T*abarī inserts at this point the narrative of the putting to death of the hostages of Jūzjān, in retaliation for the murder of the Arab hostage in Jūzjān, a much more excusable incident. Balādhur: puts it at the beginning of Qutayba's career, however, as though it belonged to the first pacification of Lower *T*ukhāristān, so that its position in *T*abarī may possibly be due to its superficial similarity with the case of Nēzak. The results of this expedition were of the greatest importance : not only was Nēzak's scheme crushed and Lower *T*ukhāristān henceforth incorporated in the Arab Empire, but also for the first time Arab authority was extended over the Jabghu and his immediate vassals in the Oxus basin. The former, exiled to Damascus, formed a valuable hostage against any attempt to regain independence, and it seems not improbable that the king of Chaghāniān was made regent for the young Jabghu (see above, p. 9), 'Abdur-Ra*h*mān was appointed governor of Balkh, in order to supervise the administration of the new province.

Qutayba had hardly returned to Merv before he was called to deal with yet another revolt. The king of Shūmān, taking advantage of the difficulties of the Arabs, or of their absence in the southern mountains, had reasserted his independence in spite of the conciliatory offers of *S*āli*h* ibn Muslim. The full weight of Qutayba's power was now employed to crush him. His stronghold was attacked with siege artillery, the king himself killed in a sortie and the garrison put to the sword. From this point Shūmān and Ākharūn gradually drop out of the Arabic narratives altogether. Qutayba then resumed his march through the Iron Gate, reduced the districts of Kish and Nasaf, and revisited Bukhārā. There seems to have been continual friction between the Arab garrison and the population (10) and it was felt that a drastic re-organisation was necessary. *T*ughshāda, though still a youth, was restored to the position ot Bukhār-Khudāh, and the leaders of the hostile party (more probably that of Khunuk Khudāh than Wardān Khudāh) were put to death. By this means, Qutayba no doubt hoped to secure compliance and docility in the native administration. *T*ughshāda had been raised to the throne by the Arabs and it might be expected that he would side with them in consequence. A more solid guarantee for the permanence of the conquest, however, was the establishment of a military colony in Bukhārā. Following the precedent set in the colonization of Merv, Arabs were lodged in the houses of the inhabitants, and it is said that the latter were encouraged to attend the Friday prayer and behave as Muslims by the distribution of a small gratuity. The Kushan merchants left their homes and property rather than comply with these orders and founded a new city outside the walls, but it is evident that the Islamization of the city was not yet so thorough as the traditions assert (**11**). The building of the Mosque and the organization of the Friday services are dated by Narshakhī in 94 A.H., which points to a further organization of the city after the capture of Samarqand. The organization of the new territories proceeded, in fact, *pari passu* with the extension and consolidation of the conquests. So long as the Arab authority was insecure in Cisoxania, it was out of the question to establish either military colonies or an elaborate administration beyond the river. Consequently, it was only now that the failure of Nēzak's revolt had definitely secured the Arab dominion in the former Ephthalite lands that it was possible to take the decisive step of settling an Arab garrison in Bukhārā. The regularity with which each step followed the last suggests that it was done according to a prearranged plan, or at least that some attention had been devoted to the question of the administration of the occupied territories in the event of the success of the military operations.

Qutayba's reorganization was not confined to the civil government, however, but extended to the army as well. Hitherto the jealousy of the Arabs for their exclusive rights as a warrior caste had strictly limited the number of Persians in the armies, apart from the clients and camp followers. Thus we are told (*T*ab. 1290. 20) that the armies of Khurāsān at this period were composed as follows : from Basra - Ahl al-'Āliya 9,000; Bakr 7,000 ; Tamīm, 10,000 ; 'Abd al Qays, 4,000 ; Azd, 10,000 : from Kūfa, 7,000 : and alongside these 47,000 Arabs only 7,000 Mawālī, commanded by *H*ayyān-an-Naba*t*ī, who is called variously a Daylamite and a native of Khurāsān. Now, however, Qutayba imposed, first on Bukhārā, and later on each successive conquest, the obligation of providing an auxiliary corps of local troops, amounting usually to some ten or twenty thousand men, to serve with the Arab armies. It is possible, if the story be true, that this was suggested by the precedent set by Sa'īd b. 'Othmān in the conquest of Samarqand, but more probable that it represents an entirely new departure in the East, though it had long been a practice in other spheres of the Arab conquests.

We are given no hint of the motives which led to the adoption of the new system, though it would seem that they must have been of some force. Possibly it was no more than a desire to keep the native armies occupied in the service of the Arabs rather than risk a revolt in their rear. *H*ajjāj and Qutayba perhaps realised too that the Arab forces by themselves, after taking four years to reduce Bukhārā alone, were insufficient to ensure success in the greater task of subduing Samarqand. Under the new system—which recalls Pan-ch'ao's famous aphorism " Use barbarians to attack barbarians "—each conquest in turn made the next more easy. The rapidity of Qutayba's later conquests in contrast with the early period is thus explained. It is just possible that in this plan Qutayba had an ulterior motive as well : the formation of a Persian army, trained on the same lines as the Arab forces, but more devoted to the person of the governor and able to take his part against the Arabs. How very nearly this plan succeeded, even in Qutayba's own case, the sequel was to show.

The practice of raising native levies, once started, appears to have become general in Khurāsān. We have no information as to when the local forces of Khurāsān and Lower Tukhāristān were incorporated in the army, nor in what proportions, but we have frequent evidence of their presence and increasing prestige in the wars of the next forty years (12). On the other hand, though contingents from the towns of Sogdiana were used by later governors if they were available, as in 106 and 112 A.H., in view of the weaker hold of the Arabs on Trans-oxania Sogdian troops never formed a regular division of the Arab forces up to the end of the Umayyad period. This distinction between the two subject Iranian groups became, as will be seen, of some importance when the 'Abbāsid propaganda began to tamper with the loyalty of the armies of Khurāsān.

While Qutayba was occupied with the new organiza-tion of Bukhārā, a detached force, sent under 'Abdur-Rahmān from Kish to Samarqand to exact from Tarkhūn the tribute agreed upon in the previous year, successfully accomplished its mission. 'Abdur-Rahmān, after restoring the hostages to Tarkhūn, rejoined his brother at Bukhārā, whence they returned to Merv for the winter.

One important vassal of Tukhāristān, who had long been a thorn in the side of Hajjāj, still remained unsub-dued. This was Rutbīl or Zunbīl, the Turkish ruler of Zābulistān (13). In 91, the viceroy united Sijistān to the province of Khurāsān, with instructions to Qutayba to undertake a campaign in person against Rutbīl. In the following year, therefore, the expeditions into Trans-oxania were interrupted, and the army again marched southwards. To Qutayba's great relief (for he disliked to undertake a campaign against this formidable foe who had made Sijistān " an ill-omened frontier ")

Rutbīl hastened to tender his submission, and at the same time sent an embassy to convey his homage to the Emperor of China (14). Recognition of Arab suzerainty over Zābulistān involved of course only the payment of a fixed tribute, and no attempt was made at a permanent occupation.

Meanwhile a serious situation had arisen in Sughd. The merchants and nobles of Samarqand had resented the weakness of their king and the payment of tribute : in Qutayba's absence the party for resistance à *outrance* gained the upper hand, and Tarkhūn, deposed on the ground of incapacity, committed suicide. The choice of the electors fell on Ghūrak (15), a prince of whom we would gladly have known more. Under the ever increasing difficulties with which he was confronted during his twenty-seven years of rule, his consummate handling of the most confused situations shows him to have been at once statesman and patriot, and preserved his kingdom from repeated disaster. The action of the Sughdian nobles, however, the Arabic account of which is confirmed by the Chinese records, constituted a challenge to Arab pretensions which Qutayba could not be slow in answering. These considerations clearly disprove the partial tradition of Abū 'Ubayda (Bal. 422), to the effect that Qutayba treacherously attacked Khwārizm and Samarqand in spite of the treaties of Sa'īd ibn 'Othmān, and the argument based upon it by van Vloten in *La Domination Arabe*, must also, in consequence, be somewhat modified.

The winter of 93/711, therefore, was spent in preparations for an expedition against Samarqand, but before the opening of the campaigning season, Qutayba received a secret mission from the Khwārizm Shāh, who offered to become tributary if the Arabs would rid him of his rebellious brother Khurrazādh. Qutayba agreed, and after publicly announcing his intention of invading Sughd, suddenly appeared at Hazārasp. The followers of the Khwārizm Shāh were persuaded to offer no resistance for this year, at least, and accepted the

terms, which included, in accordance with the new
scheme, the provision of a corps of 10,000 ablebodied
men as well as the usual tribute.   Qutayba remained at
the capital **(16)** until the army was collected, while
'Abdur-Rahmān was employed, according to Tabarī, in
reducing the king of Khāmjird, who from the parallel
account in Balādhurī is to be identified either with
Khurrazādh, or at least with his party.   The Persian
Tabarī adds a long and doubtless legendary narratve
of his surrender.   Four thousand prisoners were taken
and butchered, probably by order of the Khwārizm Shāh.

The later history of Khwārizm under Qutayba's rule
is an unhappy one.   His first governor Iyās b. 'Abdullah,
proved too weak for his post, and on Qutayba's withdrawal the Khwārizmians rose in revolt and put to death
the king who had betrayed them.   Iyās was recalled in
disgrace, together with the Persian Hayyān an-Nabañ,
who had been associated with him, and Qutayba's
brother 'Abdullah (in Balādhurī 'Ubaydullah) was
appointed as temporary regent until, after the capture
of Samarqand, a strong force under al-Mughīra b.
'Abdullah could be sent to effect a reconquest. Qutayba's
retribution on this occasion exceeded even the terror of
Paykand and Shūmān.   We are told by Al-Bīrūnī that
the educated classes and more cultured elements in
Khwārizm were slaughtered almost to extinction.   He
refers this by implication to the second expedition of
Qutayba (though it does not appear that the governor
led the expedition in person), which is borne out by what
we know of Qutayba's methods in similar cases, while
there is no instance in his career of such an action on a
first conquest.   It was in all probability the educated
classes (including no doubt the hierarchy) who led the
revolt against the traitor king and thus met with the
severest punishment.   The dynasty, however, was
maintained, and it is not improbable that the Arab colony
of which we hear shortly afterwards was settled in
Khwārizm at the same time **(17)**.

The booty from the first expedition into Khwārizm was enough to satisfy Qutayba's troops, who demanded to be allowed to return to their homes, but a sudden thrust at Samarqand promised such success that Qutayba and his leaders decided to make the attempt. The Sughdian army had apparently been disbanded, and under cover of a false movement of the advance guard, the Arabs marched directly on Samarqand. The advance guard under ' Abdur-Raḥmān numbered 20,000 men, while the main body included the new Persian contingents from Khwārizm and Bukhārā. The march occupied only a few days and the slight resistance encountered did not prevent the Arabs from proceeding at once to invest the city. Ghūrak conducted the defence with vigour, however, and appealed to Shāsh and Farghānā for assistance, reminding them that Samarqand was the bulwark of the Jaxartes valley. A strong force was despatched from Shāsh with the intention of making a surprise attack on the Arab camp, but was ambushed at night by a picked troop of Arabs and almost annihilated. This reverse, together with the continuous bombardment to which they were subjected, disheartened the Sughdians, but the wall had been breached and an entrance almost effected by the Arabs, stoutly assisted by their new Iranian divisions, before Ghūrak sued for peace. Qutayba's demands were unexpectedly light—an annual tribute, stated in widely varying amounts, and a strong corps of Sughdians, together with a stipulation that the city should be cleared of its fighting men while the Arabs built a mosque and celebrated the ritual prayers. Once within the gates, however, Qutayba refused to restore the city to Ghūrak : a strong garrison was established in the citadel, under the command of 'Abdur-Raḥmān (so Ya'qūbī ; in Tabarī 'Abdullah) and drastic orders were issued excluding all unbelievers except under strict surveillance, doubtless with the intention of avoiding a repetition of the friction that had occurred at Bukhārā. Ghūrak either could not or would not place himself in

the humiliating position of Tughshāda, and with his
retinue, accompanied possibly by the merchants, withdrew
from Samarqand altogether and built a new city, Faran-
kath, some four farsakhs distant in the direction of
Ishtīkhan (18). Qutayba's double-dealing on this
occasion, however, tarnished his reputation among both
Persians and Arabs, far more than his severity to Paykand
and Khwārizm, and left a rankling memory in Sughd.
In order to avoid the stigma of treachery attaching to
their hero the Bāhilite tradition relates this expedition
in an entirely different version (19). Qutayba, we are
told, after marching down the right bank of the Oxus
and collecting his army at Bukhārā, advanced to Rabinjān where he was met by the Sughdians under Ghūrak,
supported by the troops of Shāsh and Farghāna and the
Turks. The enemy retired on Samarqand but engaged
in constant rearguard actions, the city being finally
entered by force after a decisive battle in the suburbs.
Though this account is at first sight borne out to some
extent by Ghūrak's own narrative in his letter to the
Emperor of China, in which he claims an intitial success
against the Arabs, but was unable to prevent their
advance, both statements must be regarded as exaggerations in opposite interests. At all events it is quite
certain that none but Sughdian troops were involved at
first.

A further development of the Bāhilite tradition has
given rise to some controversy. According to this,
Ghūrak appealed for help not only to Shāsh but also to
the Khāqān, and the squadron sent from Shāsh appears
as a force of Turks, commanded by a son of the Khāqān.
This is, of course, an obvious exaggeration on the former
narrative. In the Turkish Orkhon inscriptions, however,
an expedition under the prince Kül-tegin into Sogdiana
" to organize the Sogdian people " is mentioned, following
on a successful campaign against the Türgesh in 710/711.
Marquart endeavours to prove that this expedition
occurred in 712 and is, in fact, corroborated by the

Bāhilite tradition. Professor Houtsma has raised several objections to this view, the most important being that the chronology of the inscriptions has to be manipulated to allow of this date, as the natural date to assume from the context is at latest 711. These, together with the considerations mentioned above, render Marquart's hypothesis absolutely untenable.

A second suggestion has been put forward by Professor Barthold, to which, however, Professor Houtsma's objections would apply with equal force (20). In the narrative of the historian Ya'qūbī (II. 344), there is a brief notice as follows : " Qutayba appointed his brother 'Abdur-Raḥmān ibn Muslim governor of Samarqand, but the men of Samarqand treacherously revolted against him, and Khāqān, king of the Turks, attacked him also. He wrote to Qutayba, but Qutayba waited until the winter cleared, then marched to join him and routed the army of the Turks." Professor Barthold takes the view, therefore, that this is the expedition referred to in the inscriptions, and attributes the failure of the Turks to the disastrous effects of a winter campaign in a devastated land, which so severely disabled them that they could not face the formidable army that took the field under Qutayba in the spring. It is questionable, however, how far Ya'qūbī's narrative may be trusted. None of the other historians give the slightest hint of this invasion, nor were the results such as we should expect after a Sughdian revolt. There was no ruthless reconquest, no stamping out of rebellion in blood. Neither does the general tenor of Ya'qūbī's accounts of Qutayba inspire confidence. They are not only confused in detail and chronology—the capture of Samarqand, for instance, is dated 94 A.H.—but in some cases are taken from what we know to be the Bāhilite tradition, and in others, such as the narrative under discussion and the account of the conquest of Khwārizm, follow a tradition which seems irreconcilable with our other information. While it cannot be said definitely therefore, that Ya'qūbī's

statements in this case contain no truth, it is certainly
preferable to regard them as a later development of the
narrative, on the lines of the Bāhilite tradition.

If the chronological objections raised by Professor
Houtsma are sound, there remains still a third possible
solution, which, however, as there is no corroborative
evidence from either the Arabic or Chinese sources, must
remain nothing but a hypothesis. It is surely quite
tenable that Kül-tegin's " organization of the Sogdian
people " had something to do with the deposition of
Tarkhūn and appointment of Ghūrak. With Sogdian
trade playing the most important part which we know
in the Turkish lands, it would be well worth while to try
to prevent the Arabs from obtaining control over it.
The very unexpectedness of the description given to this
expedition shows clearly that there was some motive for
" organization " and it is difficult to see what other
motive there could have been. These circumstances
would render it quite probable that Ghūrak did, in fact,
appeal to the Khāqān for assistance against the Arabs,
but it seems that the growing power of the Türgesh
barred the way into Sogdiana against the Northern
Khanate for the remainder of its short existence.

By the conquest of Samarqand Qutayba finally established his position in Transoxania. It must not be
assumed, however, as many of the Arab historians give
the impression of assuming, that the holding of Samarqand
meant the conquest of Sughd. All that had been done
was to settle an Arab garrison in a country as yet
unfriendly. It was the duty of the commanders at
Samarqand gradually to extend their authority over the
the whole district of Sughd by expeditions and razzias
(21). There was thus a radical difference between the
conquest of Bukhārā and that of Samarqand. The
former was the result of a series of campaigns in which
the resources of the country had been exhausted and the
province annexed piecemeal. The whole population had
become subjects of the Arabs and were under constant

surveillance : Tughshāda himself held his rank on suffer-
ance and was compelled to maintain at least an outward
show of loyalty. But Samarqand had been captured
in one swift thrust; Sughd as a whole was still unsubdued
and only from policy acknowledged the suzerainty of the
Arabs for the time being. " Ghūrak at Ishtīkhan was
free to turn either to the Arabs or to the Turks " (18).
Nevertheless in the years that followed there is evidence
that friendly relations were formed between the Arab
garrison and many of the local leaders and inhabitants
(22). The whole country, however, had suffered terribly
in the constant invasions and counter invasions. A
contemporary poet gives a vivid picture of its dissipated
wealth, its ruined and desolate lands :

> " Daily Qutayba gathers spoil, increasing our wealth with new
> wealth : A Bāhilite who has worn the crown till the hair that was
> black has whitened. Sughd is subdued by his squadrons, its
> people left sitting in nakedness . . .   As oft as he lights in a land,
> his horse leave it furrowed and scarred."

The Expeditions into the Jaxartes Provinces.

It might perhaps have been expected that Qutayba's
next object after the capture of Samarqand would be to
establish Arab authority in Sughd as firmly as had been
done in Bukhārā. It would probably have been better
in the end had he done so, but for the moment the attrac-
tions of the " forward policy " which had already proved
so successful were too strong. Instead of concentrating
on the reduction of Sughd, it was decided to push the
frontiers of the Empire further into Central Asia, and
leave the former to be carried out at leisure. Qutayba
therefore crossed to Bukhārā, where 20,000 levies from
Khwārizm, Bukhārā, Kish, and Nasaf had been summoned
to meet him, and marched into Sughd.   If there was a
Turkish army wintering in the country, it offered no
considerable resistance to the advance of the Arabs.
In Sughd Qutayba divided his forces into two corps.
The Persian levies were sent in the direction of Shāsh,

while he himself with the Arabs marched on Khujanda and Farghāna. Our information is brief and lacking in detail. Of the northern expedition we are told only that they captured Shāsh and burnt the greater part of it. Qutayba's own force had to overcome some resistance at Khujanda, but eventually reached Kāsān, where it was rejoined by the other. The geographers refer also to a battle fought by Qutayba at Mīnak in Ushrūsana, but against whom is not clear (**23**). Tabarī (1440. 7) preserves a tradition that Qutayba appointed an Arab resident, 'Isām b. 'Abdullah al-Bāhilī, in Farghāna. If this is true, as seems not unlikely, the appointment was probably made during this year. The details of the tradition are quite unacceptable, however. No Arab governor would ever have taken up his residence in a hill-pass in the remotest district of Farghāna, completely cut off from his fellow-countrymen. One of Balādhurī's authorities carries this or a similar tradition further by crediting Qutayba with the establishment of Arab colonies as far as Shāsh and Farghāna. Here again at most only temporary military outposts can be in question. On the other hand, the extraordinary success achieved by the Arabs on this expedition is apt to be overlooked, and Qutayba might well have imagined, as he returned to Merv, that the latest conquests were as permanently annexed to Khurāsān as Samarqand and Khwārizm.

The helplessness of their Turkish suzerain in face of the victorious Arabs, however, caused a revival in Transoxania of the tradition of Chinese overlordship. Appeals to the Khāqān were of no avail, and in the minds of the Sogdian princes, seeking for some counterpoise to the rapid extension of the Arab conquests, the idea of appealing directly to the Emperor was slowly maturing. Though no definite steps in this direction had as yet been taken, some inkling of it may have reached Qutayba. The Arabs were now familiar with China through the sea-borne trade of the Persian Gulf and at least after, if not before, their conquest of the cities which were already becoming the headquarters of Central Asian commerce, must have become aware of the close commercial relations which these cities maintained with China. Under these circumstances, Qutayba (or possibly *H*ajjāj) decided to send a mission overland to the Chinese court, possibly to prevent their intervention in the West, but more probably with the intention of promoting trade relations. As the princes of Sogdiana and *T*ukhāristān were much more alive to the advantages of preserving their commerce and to the dangers which might befall it under the new government than the Arabs could have been, it was probably on their suggestion that the embassy was sent. They would, of course, have no difficulty in persuading governors of the character of *H*ajjāj and Qutayba that their own interests also lay in safeguarding and encouraging the trade which brought such wealth to Transoxania. If the intervention of the Turks had been caused by their concern for Sogdian trade, it became doubly important for the Arabs to show their practical interest in its welfare. Apart from the immediate gain to the treasury which would accrue, such an action might reasonably be expected to secure the acquiescence of the Sogdians in Arab rule. The date of the mission is fixed as 713 by the Chinese records, which add also that in spite of the refusal of the envoys to perform the customary kow-tow it was favourably received by the Emperor. Both statements are confirmed by *T*abarī's remark that the leader was sent to Walīd on his return, which must therefore be dated between the death of *H*ajjāj and the end of 714 (**24**). Unfortunately the Arab records of the mission have been confused with the legendary exploits of Qutayba two years later, becoming so disfigured in the process as to be almost worthless. The wisdom of this step must have been justified by its results, though there are no effects apparent in our histories and the relentless march of Chinese policy was not affected. This embassy is mentioned by the Arabic historians as if it were an isolated incident, but it was, as I have shown elsewhere (**25**), only the first of many such sent by the governors of Khurāsān to maintain friendly relations with the Chinese court. It cannot be doubted that in the majority of cases at least the object of these missions was commercial, particularly where joint embassies were sent with one or other of the Sogdian principalities.

In the following year 95/714 the raids on the Jaxartes provinces were renewed. It would seem on comparing Balādhurī's account with Tabarī that Qutayba made Shāsh his headquarters and worked northwards as far as Isbījāb. The prince of Shāsh appealed to China for assistance, but without effect (26). Qutayba's plan therefore was to follow up the important trade-route which led from Turfan down the Ili valley, along the northern edge of the Thian-Shan mountains, through Tokmak and Tarāz into Shāsh and Samarqand. Though the economic importance of controlling this trade-route may have had its part in this decision, especially in view of their new patronage of Sogdian trade, it is probable that this was less in the mind of the Arabs than its strategic value as the road by which the Central Asian Turks debouched on Transoxania. Towards the end of the summer, the expeditions were abruptly interrupted by the news of the death of Hajjāj, which had occurred in Shawwāl (June). Deeply affected by the loss of his patron and not a little uncertain of the effect on his own fortunes, Qutayba disbanded the army, sending garrisons to Bukhārā, Kish, and Nasaf, and returned to Merv. Walīd, however, allayed his fears by an encouraging letter, and made his province independent of 'Irāq. But the death of Hajjāj had affected Khurāsān too deeply for such a simple remedy. The Arabs had gained wealth in their expeditions, they were weary of the constant campaigns and anxious to enjoy the comforts of peace. Factional feeling was merely slumbering, and a new element of unrest had been added by a Kūfan corps under Jahm b. Zahr, which had been transferred to Khurāsān from India by Hajjāj in his last year. All parties among the Arabs were alienated from Qutayba ; even Qays had been estranged by his highhanded action in the first place with the house of Al-Ahtam and again by his feud with Wakī' b. Abī Sūd, the chief of Tamīm (27) ; moreover, they were suspicious of his medizing tendencies. Amongst the Persians he was popular, but Hayyān an-Nabaṭī, though restored to his position in command of the Persian troops, had not forgiven Qutayba for his disgrace at Khwārizm. It seems extraordinary that the general himself should have been blind to any internal danger and was entirely confident in the loyalty of his army.

On re-opening the campaign in 96/715, therefore, his only precautions consisted in the removal of his family and personal property from Merv to Samarqand and the posting of a guard on the Oxus, in view of a possible restoration to favour of Yazīd b. Muhallab. It is unlikely that Qutayba could have had in mind the possibility of Walīd's death ; what he feared was more probably a *rapprochement* between the Caliph and his heir Sulaymān, who was his bitter enemy.

The object of this last campaign was probably the complete subjugation of Farghāna. Having established his authority over the important section of the Middle Jaxartes and its trade route, it remained now to round off his conquests by extending it also over the central trade route between Farghāna and Kashgaria. The account which Tabarī intends to convey, however, is that Qutayba marched first into Farghāna and from there led an expedition against Kashgar, with complete success. In an article of mine published in the *Bulletin of the School of Oriental Studies* (II. 467 ff.), all our evidence for this expedition has been critically discussed, and shown to be against the authenticity of the tradition. It is unnecessary, therefore, to do more than summarise very briefly the arguments there put forward. (1) None of the historians earlier than or contemporary with Tabarī contain any reference to a raid on Kashgar, and even Tabarī's own statement is not borne out by the authorities on which it professedly rests. Only one of these relates an expedition to Kashgar, and that under the command of an unknown leader. (2) The interval between the opening of the campaign and the death of Qutayba in Farghāna in August or September does not allow time for such an expedition, especially in view of the mutinous attitude of the army after the death of the Caliph. (3) The Chinese account of Arab interference in Farghāna cannot refer, for chronological reasons, to Qutayba's expedition, and in any case is silent on any attack on Kashgaria.

That an expedition of this sort should have been attributed to Qutayba is not surprising, in view of the tradition of the embassy to China, and of the great renown which attached to his memory. Later tradition (28) recounted that Hajjāj pledged the governorship of China to the first to reach it of his two governors in the East, Muhammad b. Qāsim and Qutayba. " Sīn " was, of course, not the sharply defined country of our days, but rather a loose term for the Far East, including even the Turkish lands in the North-East. Qutayba had probably done little more than make preparations for his campaign, perhaps to the extent of sending out minor raiding expeditions, when the news of the death of Walīd brought everything to a standstill.

The historians give the most contradictory accounts of the events that followed ; according to Balādhurī the new Caliph Sulaymān confirmed Qutayba in his command but gave permission to the army to disband. Tabarī's narrative, with which Ya'qūbī's in general agrees, is fully discussed by Wellhausen (274 ff.), together with a valuable analysis of Qutayba's position. The story of his highhanded negotiations with Sulaymān is too well known to need repetition. Finding the army disinclined to follow him, he completely lost his head and roused the mutiny in which he was killed. The Persian levies, who were inclined to side with him, were dissuaded by Hayyān an-Nabatī, and at the last only his own family and bodyguard of Sogdian princes remained faithful.

The death of Qutayba marked not merely the end of the Arab conquests in Central Asia for a quarter of a century, but the beginning of a period of retrogression. Under Wakī' b. Abī Sūd, his successor (**29**), the armies melted away. Mukhallad, the son of Yazīd b. Muhallab and his lieutenant in Transoxania, carried out summer raids on the villages of Sughd, but an isolated attempt on the Jaxartes provinces by 'Omar's governor, Al-Jarrāh b. 'Abdullah, met with ignominious failure. It is possibly to this that the tradition, mentioned by Barthold (*Turkestan* 160), of the disaster met with by a Muslim army refers. On the other hand an embassy was sent in the name of the Caliph to renew relations with the Chinese court, and a third in concert with the kingdoms of Tukhāristān and Samarqand, etc., during the reign of 'Omar (**25**). There is mention also of an expedition into Khuttal which regained some territory. But it was Qutayba, with Hajjāj at his back, who had held his conquests together, and when he disappeared there was neither leader nor organisation to take his place. The history of the next decade clearly shows how loose and unstable was the authority of the Arabs. It was force that had made the conquests, and only a settled policy of force or conciliation could hold them. The first was absent. " Qutayba in chains at the world's end is more terrible to us than Yazīd as governor in our very midst " is the graphic summary put into the mouths of the conquered, while of Rutbīl, king of Zābulistān, we are told expressly that after the death of Hajjāj " he paid not a cent of tribute to any of the governors of Sijistān on behalf of the Umayyads nor on behalf of Abū Muslim." (**30**).

Nor was 'Omar's policy a true policy of conciliation, based as it was not on the maintenance of the Arab conquests but on the complete evacuation of Transoxania. His orders to that effect were of course indignantly rejected by the Arab colonists in Bukhārā and Samarqand, but together with his appointment of the feeble and ineffective 'Abdur-Ra*h*mān b. Nu'aym al-Qushayrī as governor, such a policy was naturally construed by the Sogdians as mere weakness, and an invitation to regain their independence. In addition to the embassies to China, to be related in the next chapter, and possibly also some negotiations with the Türgesh, Ghūrak sought to win back his capital by playing on 'Omar's piety. The Caliph sent envoys to the princes of Sogdiana calling on them to accept Islām, and Ghūrak, outwardly professing his adherence, sent a deputation to 'Omar urging that as "Qutayba dealt with us treacherously and tyrannically, but God has now caused justice and equity to reign" the city should be restored to the Sughdians. The commonsense of the judge appointed to try the case on 'Omar's instructions by the governor of Samarqand, Sulaymān b. Abi's-Sarī (himself a mawlā), solved the problem in an eminently practical manner, and we are told that his decision, so far from being "malicious," was satisfactory to both the Arabs and the Sughdians, if not perhaps to Ghūrak. Beyond the remission of kharāj, it is doubtful whether 'Omar's administration benefited the subject peoples in the slightest, and the reaction which followed his brief reign only aggravated the situation. Already before its close the Sughdians had withdrawn their allegiance (**31**).

Thus within six years from the death of Qutayba, much of his work was undone. He had laid the foundations on which the later rule of Islām was built, and laid them well, though his own superstructure was too flimsy to withstand the tempests of the years ahead. But the fault was not entirely, perhaps not even chiefly, the fault of the builder. He was snatched away before his work was done, even if in his latter years he tended to neglect everything else for military glory. As we shall see, there was no peace in Transoxania until other men arose, great and strong enough to adopt and carry out the best of his plans. The ruthlessness and ferocity of his conquests, however, have been much exaggerated. He was always ready to use diplomacy rather than force if it offered any hope of success, so much so that his lenience was misconstrued on occasion by both friends and foes. Only in cases of treachery and revolt his punishment came swift and terrible. That he did not hesitate to take vengeance on his private enemies is to say no more than that he was an Arab. It was not without reason that in later days the Muslims of Central Asia added Qutayba's name to the roll of martyrs and that his tomb in Farghāna became a favourite place of pilgrimage (**32**).

To sum up the position in Central Asia in the years immediately following Qutayba's conquests :—

(1) Lower *T*ukhāristān and Chaghāniān formed an integral part of the Arab Empire.

(2) *T*ukhāristān, now in the decay of its power, was held as a vassal state, together with the Transoxine provinces of Khuttal, Kumādh, etc., where, however, the Arab authority was much weaker.

(3) In Sogdiana, Bukhārā was regarded as a permanent conquest and gradually colonized ; *S*ughd was still hostile territory held by strong outpost garrisons in Samarqand and Kish, connected to Bukhārā by minor posts.

(4) Khwārizm as a military power was negligible and was permanently colonized.

(5) The kingdoms beyond the Jaxartes remained independent, hostile, and relatively strong, supported by the Turkish power to the North East and also by the intervention of China.

(6) Ushrūsana, though unsubdued, does not seem to have offered any obstacle to the passage of Arab armies.

(7) The existing dynastic houses were everywhere maintained, as the representatives of the conquered peoples and vehicle of the civil administration. The actual administrative and financial authority in their

territories, however, passed to the Wāli, or agent of the Arab governor of Khurāsān (33).

NOTES

1. Chav. Doc. 42, 282 f. : Marquart Chronologie 15 : Tabarī II. 1078, 1080.
2. As was suggested by Prof. Houtsma, Gotting. Gelehrt. Anz., 1899, 386–7.
3. Suggested readings in Barthold, Turkestan, p. 71 n. 5, and p. 76.
4. Tab. 1184 f., 1195 : Chav. Doc. 172 : Hamadhānī, Kitāb al-Buldān (Bibl. Geog. Arab. V) 209. 7 : cf. Tab. 1874.
5. Narshakhī 8, 15, 30, 37, 44 : Tab. 1199. 1 : Ya'qūbī Hist. II. 342. 9.   Cf. Marquart, Chronologie 63 and Barthold, Arab. Quellen 7.
6. Hamāsa, ed. Freytag, I. 349.
7. Narshakhī 8. 15.
8. Tab. 1207. 16 : cf. Ya'qūbī loc. cit.   On the Arab method of crucifixion, Nöldeke Z.D.M.G. LVI (1902) 433 ; cf. Tab. 1691 and Dīnawarī 336. 18.
9. Detailed accounts of this are readily accessible in " The Heart of Asia ", and " The Caliph's Last Heritage " by Sir Mark Sykes, the latter in a richly imaginative vein.   Very full geographical data are given by Marquart, Ērānshahr 219 f.
10. Narsh. 46. 12, 50. 15.
11. E.g. Narsh. 58. 5.   On the new city, Barthold Turkestan 110 f.
12. E.g. Tab. 1544. 9, 1600 ff.
13. On this dynasty see Ērānshahr 37 f., 248 ff. and de Goeje in W.Z.K.M. XVI (1902) 192–195.
14. Ya'qūbī Geog. 283 : Chav. Doc. 161.
15. The pronunciation of this name, usually pointed Ghūzak, is fixed by the Chinese transcription U-le-kia (Chav. Doc. 136).
16. On the city of Khwārizm (Fīl, Kath) see Sachau " Zur Geschichte usw. von Khwārizm " pp. 23–25.
17. Tab. 1252 f., 1525 : Bal. 421 : Al-Bīrūnī, " Chronology of Ancient Nations " (trans. Sachau, London 1879) pp. 41 f.   Prof. Barthold is inclined to regard Al-Bīrūnī's narrative as fictitious (perhaps intended to account for the absence of written records of Khwārizm dating from pre-Muslim times ?) cf. " Turkestan " p. 1.
18. Barthold, Arab. Quellen 21 f.
19. Tab. 1247 f., 1249.   For Ghūrak's latter, Chav. Doc. 204 f.
20. Marquart, Chronologie 5 ff. : Barthold, Arab. Quell. 11 f. : Houtsma as note 2 above.
21. Cf. Tab. 1418 : Bal. 425.
22. Tab. 1365. 8, 1518, 1542. 1.
23. Ibn Hawqal 383 ; Istakhrī 328. 4.   The latter's statement that Qutayba here beleaguered the Afshīn of Ushrūsana is almost certainly due to the omission of some words or perversion of the text.   On the other hand, there could not be, as in Ibn Hawqal's account, any question of Musaw-wida (" Black Robes ") in the ordinary sense of the term as early as 94 A.H. and above all in Ushrūsana.

The absence of any reference to levies from Sughd in this expedition would seem to favour Prof. Barthold's theory of a Sughdian rising in co-operation with the Turks. The evidence in favour of an accidental omission is, however, very strong. At this point Tabarī's narratives, in contrast to the preceding period, become extremely brief. The levies from the four states mentioned met Qutayba at Bukhārā and marched with him into Sughd. Naturally the Sughdian levies would have awaited his arrival there. Had the omission been intentional it would be difficult to explain why Tabarī did not include some account of the reasons why Sughdian troops were not summoned. In any case it is certain that Qutayba would not have left a hostile Sughdian army in his rear, and they must therefore have taken part in the march to the Jaxartes.

24. Cordier, Hist. gen. de la Chine, I. 460 : Wieger 1642 : Tab. 1280. 3.
25. Bulletin of the School of Oriental Studies, II. 619 ff. For another view of these embassies see Bretschneider, Mediaeval Researches (1910), II. 247 f.
26. Hirth, Nachworte 81.
27. Bal. 425 f. : Ya'qūbī, Hist. II. 354 : Wellhausen, Arab. Reich 275.
28. Ya'qūbī, Hist. II. 346. 7.
29. See his character-sketch in Wellhausen 277.
30. Bal. 401. 5 : Tab. 1353.
31. Tab. 1364 f., 1356. 13, 1364. 13, 1421. 7, 1418. 13 : Bal. 422, 426.
32. Narsh. 57. 4 : Fażā'il Balkh, ap. Schefer, Chrest. Persane, I. 71. 2.
33. Sachau, Khwārizm I, 29 : Barthold, Turkestan 189.

IV. THE TURKISH COUNTERSTROKE (1)

THE princes of Transoxania had so long been accustomed to regard the Arabs as mere marauders that it was some time before they could realise the loss of their independence. Though necessity forced them at first to adopt a conciliatory spirit (as, for example, in their acceptance of Islām under 'Omar II), they were dismayed to find all the machinery of permanent occupation set in motion, and their authority flouted by tactless and greedy Arab officials. Such a state of affairs was tolerable only in the absence of any countering force. The situation was not stationary for long, however ; even before Qutayba's death other and disturbing factors had begun to enter. Our best clue to the complications in Transoxania during this period is the attitude of Ghūrak, king of Sughd, of whose movements, fortunately, sufficient indications have been preserved. In maintaining a precarious balance between the Türgesh and the Arabs, his true statesman's instinct seldom misled him in judging how and when to act to advantage throughout his troubled reign. In addition to this we have the evidence, unreliable in detail but confirmatory in the mass, of the embassies sent by the subject principalities to the Chinese court. Doubtless they were despatched in the guise of commercial missions and in many cases were truly so, but that they frequently possessed a political character can hardly be denied. The dates of these embassies as given in the authorities translated by Chavannes fall naturally into four periods. In the following list all embassies have been omitted in which the Arabs are known to have participated or whose object is known to have had no connection with the Arab conquests, as well as those which appear to be duplicated, and those from the minor states :

NUMBER OF EMBASSIES FROM :—

1.	717-731	Sughd 11,	Tukhāristān	5,	Bukhārā 2,	Arabs	4.
2.	732-740	,, none	,,	2	,, none	,,	1 (733).
3.	741-747	,, 4	,,	3	,, 1	,,	4
4.	750-755	,, 4	,,	2	,, 3	,,	6

These four periods, as will be seen, closely correspond to the fluctuations of Arab authority in Transoxania.

In the same year, 713, that Qutayba first led his army across the Jaxartes, a new era of westward expansion opened in China with the accession of Hiuen-Tsong. In 714 the Chinese intervened in the affairs of the Ten Tribes and obtained their immediate submission, while in the following year they restored the deposed king of Farghāna. In 716, on the death of Me-chu'o, Khan of the Northern Turks, the powerful tribes of the Türgesh asserted their independence, and under their chief Su-Lu established, with Chinese assistance, a new kingdom in the Ili basin. The princes of Transoxania eagerly sought to profit by these developments to free themselves from the Arab yoke. In 718 a joint embassy was sent to China by Tughshāda, Ghūrak, Narayāna king of Kumādh, and the king of Chaghānian. The first three presented petitions for aid against the Arabs, which are given in full in Chavannes' *Documents*. Tughshāda asked that the Türgesh might be ordered to attack the Arabs, Ghūrak related the capture of Samarqand and asked for Chinese troops, Narayāna complained of the seizure of all his treasures by the Arabs and asked that representations might be made to induce them to remit their crushing taxation. It is significant that the king of Chaghānian, acting for his suzerain, the Jabghu of Tukhāristān, did not compromise himself by joining in these requests. But beyond " fair words " the son of Heaven took no action, and no Chinese forces appeared West of the Jaxartes, in spite of the repeated entreaties addressed by the princes to their self-elected suzerain.

The Türgesh, however, were not long in intervening on their own account. Whatever opportunity the Arab government had to pacify the Sughdians was lost by a succession of incompetent governors. Already in the reign of 'Omar II, as has been seen, they had withdrawn their allegiance from the weak 'Abdur-Raḥmān b. Nu'aym. For a moment the situation seemed to improve at the beginning of the governorship of Sa'īd " Khudhayna " (102/720) owing to the firm handling of Samarqand by his lieutenant Shu'ba b. Zuhayr. But disturbances broke out and Shu'ba was recalled, perhaps in a vain attempt to appease the insurgents. It would seem that the Sughdians appealed to the new Turkish power in the East and Su-Lu, unable to make headway against the growing influence of China, willingly seized the opportunity of diverting his armies into Transoxania. A small Türgesh force was sent under Köl-chur (called by Tabarī Kūrsūl) (2) to make common cause with the Sughdian rebels in the following spring (end of 102). Sa'īd awoke to find the whole country in arms, a Turkish force marching on Samarqand, and the local princes, with few exceptions, aiding the invaders. The Arab commanders could not rely on their levies and a small garrison at Qaṣr al-Bāhilī was evacuated only with the utmost difficulty. The tale of their relief by a small force of volunteers is one of the most spirited narratives of adventure in Tabarī. But such episodes did not affect the general success of the Turkish forces. Kūrsūl continued his advance through Sughd without opposition, avoiding Samarqand, until at last Sa'īd was roused by public reproach to march against the Turks. After a small initial success, which he refused to follow up, he was severely defeated and confined to the neighbourhood of Samarqand. The Turks were not strong enough to undertake a siege of the city, as the whole operation seems to have been little more than a reconnaissance in force combined with a raiding expedition. As the Türgesh retired, the Arab cavalry followed them up as far as Waraghsar, the head of the canal system of Sughd. Ghūrak appears to have refrained from committing himself by openly aiding the rebels, and doubtless recognised that the Arabs were not so easily to be dislodged. From the fact that Sa'īd's camp was pitched at Ishtīkhan, in close proximity to him, it may even be conjectured that he outwardly supported the Arabs.

But the new governor of 'Irāq, 'Omar b. Hubayra, was not the man to stand idly by in face of the danger that threatened Khurāsān. The weakness shown by Khudhayna and the complaints of oppression from his subjects, were sufficient reason for his recall, and Sa'īd b. 'Amr al-Harashī, a man of very different stamp, was installed in his place. The transfer may be placed in the late autumn of 103/721. The new governor's first act was to summon the rebels to submit, but a large number of nobles and merchants, with their retainers, either fearing that they could expect no mercy, or anxious to free themselves altogether from the Arab yoke, prepared to emigrate to Farghāna. Ghūrak did his utmost to persuade them to remain, but without effect ; their absence would no doubt affect the revenues, and a certain emphasis is laid on the point in Tabarī's account. Leaving hostages behind, the malcontents marched towards Farghāna and opened negotiations with the king for the occupation of 'Isām. The majority settled in the interval at Khujanda, but other parties actually entered Farghāna, and one body at least occupied a fortified position on the Zarafshān. Al-Harashī followed up his demands by marching into Sughd and encamped near Dabūsia, where he was with difficulty persuaded to stay until sufficient contingents arrived. On advancing, he was met by a messenger from the king of Farghāna, who, outwardly professing to assist the Sughdians, had secretly decided to rid himself of them by calling in the Arabs against them. Al-Harashī eagerly seized the opportunity and pressed forward, receiving the allegiance of Ushrūsana as he passed. The emigrants, although urged by their leader Karzanj either to take active measures or to submit, decided to risk a siege in Khujanda, trusting to the protection of the king of Farghāna. But when Sa'īd set about the siege in earnest, and they realised that they had been betrayed, they surrendered on unexpectedly easy terms. Sa'īd divided them, placing the nobles and merchants in a camp apart from the soldiers. By the execution of Thābit, a noble from Ishtīkhan, he provoked a revolt, under pretext of which he massacred the nobles and the troops, sparing the merchants, who numbered four hundred, only in order to squeeze them of their wealth. Tabarī's account very thinly veils al-Harashī's responsibility for this wanton act of atrocious cruelty, which could not fail to embitter the feelings of the whole population of Transoxania. It is curious that the Persian Tabarī (Zotenberg IV. 268) has an entirely different story, which is found in none of the Arabic authorities. The refugees who escaped eventually took refuge with the Khāqān of the Türgesh, where they formed a regiment (no doubt continually recruited from new emigrants) which particularly distinguished itself in the war against the Arabs (3).

The expedition to Khujanda may be put in the spring and summer of 722 (end of 103, beginning of 104), though the chronology here, and indeed for all this period, is uncertain. The piecemeal reduction of the fortresses in Sughd occupied the remainder of the year, a series of operations whose difficulty is sufficient witness to the effect of the news from Khujanda in stiffening the resistance to the Arabs. The first fortress to be attacked was that of Abghar, in which a band of the emigrants had settled. The attack was entrusted to Sulaymān b. Abi's-Sarī, with an army composed largely of native levies from Bukhārā, Khwārizm, and Shūmān, accompanied by their princes. Sulaymān persuaded the dihqān to surrender, and sent him to al-Harashī, who at first treated him well in order to counteract the effect of the massacre of Khujanda, but put him to death after recapturing Kish and Rabinjān. The most inaccessible fortress and the crowning example of Al-Harashī's perfidy were left to the last. The dihqān Subuqrī still held out in the fortress of Khuzar, to the south of Nasaf; unable to take it by force, Al-Harashī sent Musarbal b. Al-Khirrīt, a personal friend of Subuqrī, to offer him a pardon. On his surrender, he was sent to Merv and put to death, although the amnesty, it is said, had been confirmed by 'Omar b. Hubayra.

The whole of Sughd was thus once more in the hands of the Arabs. The nearer districts, Khwārizm and Bukhārā, had remained loyal and the Oxus basin seems to have been unaffected. But to make a solitude and call it peace did not suit the aims of the Arab government and Al-Harashī found that his " policy of thorough " only provided Ibn Hubayra with an excuse for superseding him. During the winter, therefore, he was replaced by Muslim b. Sa'īd al-Kilābī, who, as the grandson of Aslam b. Zur'a, came of a house long familiar with Khurāsān. The danger of the movement of revolt spreading to the Iranians of Khurāsān seems to have preoccupied the Arab government during all this period. Sa'īd Khudhayna had poisoned the too-influential Hayyān an-Nabatī on suspicion of rousing the Persians against the government and that it was felt even in Basra may be seen from Ibn Hubayra's advice to his new governor, " Let your chamberlain be one who can make peace with your mawālī." Muslim, in fact, favoured the Persians and did all in his power to appoint officials acceptable to them, the Mazdean Bahrām Sīs, for example, being appointed Marzubān of Merv (4). But all such measures were merely palliatives and could not materially affect the growing discontent in Sughd and Tukhāristān. During his first year of office it is recorded (if the narrative is not, as Wellhausen thinks, a duplicate of the raid on Farghāna in the following year) that Muslim marched across the river but was met and pushed back into Khurāsān by a Turkish army, narrowly escaping disaster. It is not improbable that the local forces were again assisted by Türgesh on this occasion.

In the following year, however, before the close of 105, a second expedition gained some success at Afshīna, near Samarqand. Meanwhile Hishām had succeeded Yazīd II as Caliph, and 'Omar b. Hubayra, whose Qaysite leanings were too pronounced, was recalled in favour of Khālid b. 'Abdullah al-Qasrī of Bajīla. The transfer took place most probably in March (724), though another account places it some months later. Muslim was now preparing an expedition into Farghāna, but the Yemenite troops at Balkh held back partly through dislike of the campaign and doubtless expecting the governor's recall. Naṣr b. Sayyār was sent with a Muḍarite force to use compulsion ; the mutinous Yemenites were defeated at Barūqān and unwillingly joined the army. It is noteworthy that troops from Chaghānian fought alongside Naṣr in this engagement. Before leaving Bukhārā Muslim learned that he was to be superseded, at the same time receiving orders to continue his expedition. Four thousand Azdites, however, took the opportunity of withdrawing. The remainder, accompanied by Sughdian levies, marched into Farghāna, crossed the Jaxartes, and besieged the capital, cutting down the fruit trees and devastating the land. Here news was brought that Khāqān was advancing against them, and Muslim hurriedly ordered a retreat. The Arabic accounts graphically describe the headlong flight of the Arabs. On the first day they retired three stages, the next day they crossed the Wādī Sabūh, closely pursued by the Türgesh ; a detachment, largely composed of mawālī, which encamped separately, was attacked and suffered heavy losses, the brother of Ghūrak being amongst the killed. After a further eight days' march, continually harassed by the light Turkish horse, they were reduced to burning all the baggage, to the value of a million dirhems. On reaching the Jaxartes the following day, they found the way barred by the forces of Shāsh and Farghāna, together with the Sughdians who had escaped from Sa'īd al-Harashī, but the desperate and

F

thirsty troops, hemmed in by the Türgesh from behind, cut their way through. The rearguard made a stand, but lost its commander. At length the remnants of the army reached Khujanda, where 'Abdur-Raḥmān b. Nu'aym took command on behalf of Asad b. 'Abdullah, and made good his retreat to Samarqand.

This disaster, which is known as the " Day of Thirst," marks a period in the history of the Arab conquests. It was practically the last aggressive expedition of the Arabs into Transoxania for fifteen years, but of much greater importance was the blow which it struck at Arab prestige. The rôles were reversed ; from now onwards the Arabs found themselves on the defensive and were gradually ousted from almost every district across the Oxus. No wonder, therefore, that the memory of the " Day of Thirst " rankled even long after it had been avenged (5). According to the Arab tradition, the Türgesh armies were led on this occasion not by Su-Lu himself, but by one of his sons. Unfortunately the accounts of Su-Lu in such Chinese works as have been translated are silent on his Western expeditions, and the Arab historians are our only authorities. The immediate result of the Arab defeat, not only in Sughd but in Tukhāristān and the southern basin as well, was to stiffen the attitude of passive resistance to the Arabs to the point at which it only needed active support to break into a general conflagration. From this time, if not before, the subject princes regarded the Türgesh as the agents of their deliverance, commissioned by China in response to the urgent entreaties they had addressed to the Emperor for aid in their struggle. We find this actually expressed in a letter sent three years later by the Jabghu of Tukhāristān, which is, in Chavannes' words "but one long cry of distress" (6). " I am loaded with heavy taxation by the Arabs ; in truth, their oppression and our misery are extreme. If I do not obtain the help of the (Chinese) Kagan . . . my kingdom will certainly be destroyed and dismembered . . . . I have been told that the

Celestial Kagan has given this order to the Kagan of the Türgesh : To you I delegate the affairs of the Far West ; you must at once send soldiers to drive out the Arabs." The point of view here expressed is of course that of the ruling princes, whose resentment at the curtailment of their authority is understandable. Besides making allowance for some natural exaggeration, it would be dangerous to assume that this was as yet fully shared by the people. In all probability, if we may judge from historical analogies, there was also a pro-Arab party in Sogdiana, who felt that the best interests of the country lay, not in an opposition whose final issue could scarcely be in doubt, but in co-operation with their new masters as far as was possible. The tragedy of the Arab administration was that by alternately giving and refusing co-operation on its side, it drove its supporters in the end to make common cause with its opponents.

But though the situation was steadily deteriorating the decisive moment had not yet come. The new governor, Asad b. 'Abdullah, seems to have seen something of the danger though factional feeling was running so high that the administration was almost helpless in face of it. He tried to continue Muslim's policy of conciliation by appointing agents of known probity. Tawba b. Abī Usayd, a mawlā who had been intendant for Muslim, and who " treated the people fairly, made himself easily accessible, dealt uprightly with the army and maintained their supplies," he persuaded to remain in office under him. Hāni' b. Hāni', the financial intendant at Samarqand, was unpopular ; he was recalled and Al-Hasan b. Abi'l-'Amarrata of Kinda, who was in sympathy with the mawālī, appointed in his place. With him was associated Thābit Qutna, who had been a leader of some repute under Sa'īd Khudhayna, " gallant warrior, distinguished poet, confidant of Yazīd b. Muhallab, and universally popular " (7). Still more significant is the fact that one of Asad's earliest actions was to renew the practice, neglected since the days of 'Omar II, of sending an embassy to the Chinese court. As before, however, the Arabs resented the favour shown to the Persians, and the military weakness of Ibn Abi'l-'Amarra*t*a roused them to open anger. Strong Turkish forces, probably guerilla bands swollen by refugees and malcontents from the wasted districts, spread over the country and appeared even before Samarqand. The governor made some show of opposition, but avoided coming to grips with them, thus intensifying his unpopularity.

Samarqand indeed was gradually becoming more and more isolated, but no assistance could be given from Khurāsān. During his three years of office Asad's attention was wholly engaged with the situation in *T*ukhāristān and the South. Even here his constant expeditions, to Gharjistān, Khuttal, and elsewhere, met with no success. Worse still, in 108/726 he found his forces in Khuttal opposed by the Khāqān with his Türgesh. The princes of *T*ukhāristān had taken to heart the lessons of the " Day of Thirst ", and the powerful chief who had already all but driven the Arabs out of Sogdiana was now called in to expel them from the Oxus basin as well. Asad visited his failure on the Mu*d*arites, whom he may have suspected of treachery, but the indignation called out by his treatment of such men as Na*s*r b. Sayyār, 'Abdur-Ra*h*mān b. Nu'aym, Sawra b. Al-*H*urr, and Al-Bakhtarī, made his recall inevitable. Nor had his measures removed the distrust and hatred of the subject peoples. The land was wasted and desolate (8), the crushing taxation was not lightened, and all Persian governors were not of the stamp of Tawba ; many of them were but too ready to rival their Arab rulers in greed and cruelty. Asad may have gained the friendship of many dihqāns (9), but that was an easier matter than to placate the population. In such an atmosphere it was only to be expected that Shī'ite and 'Abbāsid propaganda, though actively combated by the administration, found a fertile field among the Muslim converts in Khurāsān and Lower *T*ukhāristān, and was already beginning to undermine the whole fabric of Arab government.

For a moment the hopes of a radical change of policy entertained by the mawālī and the clearer-sighted Arabs were raised to the highest pitch by the appointment (in 109) of Ashras b. 'Abdullah as-Sulami, accompanied by the separation of Khurāsān from Khālid al-Qasrī's province of 'Irāq. It is unnecessary to recapitulate here the far-reaching concessions by which he hoped to secure, and actually did for a time secure the allegiance of the Sughdians, or the methods by which the local princes, especially Ghūrak, succeeded in checking the movement (10). It is generally assumed that the hostility of Ghūrak was due to the serious fall in revenue which would result. Though this was doubtless the plea put forward and accepted by Ashras it can scarcely have been the true issue. Ghūrak's aim was not to maintain himself on good terms with the Arab governors but to recover his independence. If once the people became "Arabs" all hope of success must have been lost. It was a game with high stakes and Ghūrak won. It must not be over-looked, however, that the account as we have it is traditional and may often be mistaken on the sequence of cause and effect. The astonishing reversal of the measures adopted by Ashras is more probably to be explained by pressure from above, not from below, and our tradition may really present only the popular view of the Caliph Hishām's reorganization of the financial adminis-tration (11). The Arabs resorted to brutal methods to wring the taxes from the new converts, and with incredible blindness selected the dihqāns for special indignities. It is not unlikely that Narshakhī's story of the martyrdom of native Muslims in Bukhārā is con-nected with this event, though there are many other possible explanations, such as, for example, an attempted Hārithite movement (see below, p. 76f.) The reaction swung the whole population of Transoxania, dihqāns and peasantry alike, into open rebellion. The first small

party of emigrants who quitted Samarqand, although
supported by a few Arabs, were induced to surrender and
return (**12**), but within a few months the dreaded Khāqān
with his Türgesh had joined forces with the rebels and
swept the Arabs across the Oxus. Even Bukhārā was
lost (**13**) and only Samarqand with two minor posts
on the Zarafshān, Kamarja and Dabūsia, held out.
Ghūrak, however, still supported the Arabs, as
Samarqand, although besieged, seems to have been in
no danger, while his son Mukhtār, doubtless to keep a
footing in the opposite camp, joined with the Türgesh.

The pressing danger sobered the Arabs and tempor-
arily united all parties and factions. The army was
concentrated at Āmul but for three months was unable to
cross the river in the face of the combined native and
Türgesh armies. A small body under Qaṭan b. Qutayba
which had already crossed and fortified itself before the
arrival of the Turks was beleaguered. The Turkish
cavalry even made raids on Khurāsān with an excess of
boldness which was punished by a mounted force under
Thābit Quṭna. At length Ashras got his forces across
and, joining with Qaṭan b. Qutayba, advanced on
Paykand. The enemy cut off the water supply, and had
it not been for the gallantry and self-sacrifice of Ḥārith
b. Surayj, Thābit Quṭna, and their companions, an even
greater and more irretrievable " Day of Thirst " had
resulted. In spite of their weakness, Qaṭan and the
cavalry of Qays and Tamīm charged the enemy and forced
them back, so that Ashras was able to continue his
advance towards Bukhārā. In the heavy fighting the
Muslim forces were divided, Ashras and Qaṭan gave each
other up for lost, and Ghūrak judged that the time had
come to throw in his lot with the Turks. Two days later,
however, the armies were reunited and on the retiral of
the Turks encamped at Bawādara outside the walls of
Bukhārā, whence they prepared to besiege the city.
Ghūrak also retrieved his error and rejoined Ashras.
The Khāqān withdrew towards Samarqand, but sat down

before Kamarja, expecting to take it by storm in a few
days at the most.   The Arabic narratives of these events
are confused in several places, which has given rise to
many incorrect statements, such as that Ghūrak was
beleaguered with the Arabs in Kamarja and that the
garrison consisted of Qatan and his forces.   Kamarja was
not in the neighbourhood of Paykand, as Wellhausen
states, but a few farsakhs west of Samarqand (14). When
the garrison would not yield to assault Khāqān tried
other methods.   Accompanying his expedition was
Khusrū the son of Pērōz and grandson of Yazdigird,
heir of the Sāsānid kings.   This prince was sent to parley
with the garrison, but when he claimed the restoration
of his kingdom and promised them an amnesty, it is not
surprising that the Arabs indignantly refused to hear him.
Nor would the appearance of a Sāsānid prince evoke
much enthusiasm amongst the Iranians of Transoxania.
As the Sāsānid house had taken refuge in China, however,
the presence of Khusrū might be taken as an indication
that the rebels were receiving encouragement from China
also, though the Chinese records are silent on this
expedition.   Khāqān's second proposal, that he should
hire the Arabs as mercenaries, was rejected as derisively
as the first.   The siege was then pressed with renewed
vigour, both sides putting their prisoners and hostages
to death, but after fifty-eight days Khāqān, on the advice
of the son of Ghūrak and the other Sughdian princes,
allowed the garrison to transfer either to Samarqand or
Dabūsia.   On their choosing the latter, the terms were
faithfully carried out after on exchange of hostages.

The fame of the defence of Kamarja spread far and
wide, but it brought little relief to the pressure on the
Arabs in Transoxania.   Even Khwārizm was affected
by the movement of revolt, but at the first symptoms of
open rebellion it was crushed by the local Muslims,
probably Arabs settled in the district, with the aid of a
small force despatched by Ashras.   The reference made in
Tabarī to assistance given to the rebels by the Turks is

probably to be discounted, as is done by Ibn al-Athīr.
It is of course quite possible that the movement was
instigated by the Türgesh, though no such explanation
is necessary, but if any Turks were engaged they were
probably local nomadic tribes.   Ashras seems to have
remained before Bukhārā during the winter, possibly
in Paykand ; the Türgesh probably withdrew towards
Shāsh and Farghānā.

In the following year, 730/111–112 (15), the attacks on
the army of Ashras were renewed.   The course of events
can only be gathered from the accounts given of the
difficulties experienced by the new governor, Junayd
b. 'Abdur-Raḥmān al-Murrī, in joining the army before
Bukhārā.   His guide advised him to levy a force from
Zamm and the neighbouring districts before crossing the
Oxus but Junayd refused, only to find himself after crossing put to the necessity of calling on Ashras for a bodyguard of cavalry.   This force narrowly escaped disaster
on its way to meet Junayd and fought a second severe
engagement on the return journey before reaching
Paykand.   The enemy are variously described as " men
of Bukhārā and Sughd " and " Turks and Sughdians " ;
it may therefore be assumed that they were the same
forces against whom Ashras had fought the previous
year.   Wellhausen is probably correct in supposing that
Ashras was practically beleaguered, though not in
Bukhārā.   The recapture of this city and the retiral of
Khāqān took place shortly after Junayd's arrival, in
circumstances which are not described (16).   The
attitude of Tugshāda during this episode is not recorded.
It is practically certain, however, that he remained in
Bukhārā, and after the reconquest was able to make his
peace with the Arabs, probably on the excuse of *force
majeure*.   At all events he retained his position, possibly
because Junayd thought it impolitic in the face of the
situation to victimise the nobles in the reconquered
territories and thus provoke a more stubborn resistance
in the rest of the country.   The Arabs seem to have

followed up the Turks towards Samarqand, probably to
relieve the garrison ; the two armies met again at
Zarmān, seven farsakhs from Samarqand, where the
Arabs claimed a success, one of their prisoners being a
nephew of Khāqān. From Sughd the army marched
to Tirmidh where Junayd halted for two months in the
friendly atmosphere of Chaghāniān before returning to
Merv. His intention was no doubt to make arrangements
for the pacification or reconquest of Tukhāristān and
Khuttal ; in the following year his troops were actually
engaged in this direction when the Türgesh invasion of
Sughd forced him to change his plans. Balādhurī
quotes Abū 'Ubayda for the statement that Junayd
reconquered certain districts in Tukhāristān which had
revolted.

How lightly even yet factional feeling was slumbering
was shown after the return of the army, when the
Bāhilites of Balkh had a chance to retaliate on Nasr b.
Sayyār for their discomfiture at Barūqān. Though
Junayd was prompt to punish the offending governor,
the incident throws a strong light on one cause of the
weakness of the Arabs in these campaigns.

Early in 731/112–113, the Türgesh and Sughdians
gathered their forces for the investment of Samarqand.
Ghūrak now openly joined the Khāqān. Sawra b.
Al-Hurr, the governor of Samarqand, unable to face the
enemy in the field, sent an urgent message to Junayd for
assistance. The governor hastily recalled his troops,
but crossed the river without waiting for them against
the advice of his generals. " No governor of Khurāsān,"
said al-Mujashshar b. Muzāhim, one of the ablest of the
Arab commanders, " should cross the river with less than
fifty thousand men." Accompanied only by a small
force, Junayd reached Kish, where he raised some local
levies and prepared to march on Samarqand. The enemy
in the meantime, after blocking up the water supplies
on his road, interposed their forces between Samarqand
and the army of relief. Junayd thereupon decided to

follow the direct route across the Shāwdār mountains
in the hope of avoiding an engagement, but when only
four farsakhs from Samarqand was surprised in the
defiles by Khāqān. The advance-guard was driven in
and the main body engaged in a furious struggle in which
both sides fought to a standstill. The Arabs, hemmed in
on all sides, were forced to entrench ; stragglers, refugees,
and baggage, collected near Kish, were attacked by a
detachment of Turks and severely handled. Khāqān
renewed his attacks on the camp the next day, all but
overwhelming Junayd, and settled down thereafter to
beleaguer him. In this predicament there was only one
course open to Junayd. Had his force perished, Samarq-
and would certainly have fallen in the end and two
disasters taken the place of one. He therefore adopted
the more prudent, if unheroic, course of ordering Sawra
to leave a skeleton garrison in Samarqand and march out
to join him by way of the river : Sawra, however, took
the short cut across the mountains, and was actually
within four miles of Junayd, when the Turkish forces
bore down on him. The battle lasted into the heat of
the day, when the Turks, on Ghūrak's advice it is said,
having first set the grass on fire, drew up so as to shut
Sawra off from the water. Maddened by heat and thirst,
the Arabs charged the enemy and broke their ranks,
only to perish miserably in the fire, Turks and Muslims
together. The scattered remnants were pursued by the
Turkish cavalry and of twelve thousand men scarcely
a thousand escaped. While the enemy were engaged with
Sawra, Junayd freed himself from his perilous position
in the defiles, though not without severe fighting, and
completed his march to Samarqand. Tabarī gives also
a variant account of the " Battle of the Pass," the main
difference in which is the inclusion of the Jabghu on the
side of the Turks. In view of the Arab expeditions into
Tukhāristān, it is improbable that the Jabghu, even if
he was present personally, which is doubtful, was
accompanied by any of his troops. The Persian Tabarī

also contains an entirely different version of the Battle of the Pass and the fate of Sawra. The original version is amply attested by contemporary poets, who show no mercy to Junayd. Whatever credit the Arabs gained in this battle is reflected on Nasr b. Sayyār and the mawālī. Junayd remained at Samarqand for some time, recuperating his forces, while couriers were sent to Hishām with the news of the disaster. The Caliph immediately ordered twenty thousand reinforcements from Basra and Kūfa to be sent to Khurāsān, together with a large number of weapons and a draft on the treasury, at the same time giving Junayd a free hand in enlistment.

The Turks, disappointed in their attack on Samarqand, withdrew to Bukhārā, where they laid siege to Qatan b. Qutayba. Here they were also on the natural lines of communication between Samarqand and Khurāsān. Junayd held a council, and of three alternatives, either to remain in Samarqand and await reinforcements, or to retire on Khurāsān *via* Kish and Zamm, or to attack the enemy, chose the last. But the morale of the Arabs was sadly shaken ; a garrison of eight hundred men for Samarqand was scraped together only by granting a considerable increase in their pay, while the troops openly regarded the decision to face Khāqān and the Turkish hordes as equivalent to courting destruction. Junayd now marched with the utmost circumspection, however, and easily defeated a small body of the enemy in a skirmish near Karmīnia. The following day Khāqān attacked his rearguard near Tawāwīs (on the edge of the oasis of Bukhārā), but the attack had been foreseen and was beaten off. As it was now well into November, the Türgesh were compelled to withdraw from Sogdiana, while Junayd entered Bukhārā in triumph on the festival of Mihrjān. In Chaghāniān he was joined by the reinforcements, whom he sent on to Samarqand, the remainder of the troops returning to their winter quarters.

Junayd seems to have been content with saving

Samarqand and Bukhārā. As no further expeditions are recorded of his two remaining years of office it must be assumed that the situation in Sughd remained unchanged and that the Türgesh irruptions also were suspended. Though the Arabs still held Samarqand and the territories of Bukhārā and Kish, they were in all probability confined to these, while in the southern basin their authority hardly extended beyond Balkh and Chaghāniān. Both sides may have awaited the first move by the other, but were surprised by the appearance of a new factor, which threatened the existence of Arab sovereignty in the Far East more seriously than any external danger. It is noteworthy that in his last year of office (115/733) Junayd resumed relations with the Chinese court. The Turkish title of the leader of the embassy, Mo-se-lan Tarkan, suggests that none of the ambassadors were actually Arabs, but that the governor had commissioned some dignitaries from the subject states to represent the Arab government. The only embassy recorded in this year from a native state, however, came from Khuttal. In the same year Khurāsān was visited by a severe drought and famine, and to provide for the needs of Merv, Junayd commandeered supplies from all the surrounding districts. This, added to the military disasters of the last few years and the insinuations of Shī'ite propaganda, provoked open discontent in the district which had hitherto been outwardly faithful to Merv, namely the principalities of Lower Tukhāristān. The leader of the malcontents was Al-Hārith b. Surayj, who was flogged in consequence by the governor of Balkh. The discontent flared into open revolt on the death of Junayd in Muharram 716 (Feb. 734). Hārith, assisted by the princes and people of Jūzjān, Fāryāb, and Tālaqān, marched on Balkh and captured it from Nasr b. Sayyār. The versions leave it uncertain whether Hārith defeated Nasr and then captured the city or whether he entered the city first and beat off an attempt at recapture by Nasr.

(Wellhausen's reference to the Oxus is due to his so misunderstanding the " river of Balkh " in Tab. 1560. 2.
That it refers here, as frequently, to the Dehas river is
clear from the distance to the city (2 farsakhs, whereas
the Oxus lay twelve farsakhs from Balkh) as well as from
the mention of the bridge of 'Aṭā.) From Balkh he moved
against the new governor 'Āsim b. 'Abdullah al-Hilālī,
at Merv, capturing Merv-Rūdh on the way. 'Āsim found
a large section of the inhabitants in league with Hārith,
but on his threatening to evacuate Merv and to call for
Syrian troops, the local forces rallied round him. At
the first reverse, the princes of Lower Tukhāristān
deserted Hārith, whose army fell from sixty thousand to
three thousand. He was thus reduced to making terms
with 'Āsim, but early in the following year renewed his
revolt. 'Āsim, hearing that Asad b. 'Abdullah was on
the way as his successor, began to intrigue with Hārith
against him. The plan miscarried, however ; Hārith
seized the governor and held him to ransom, so that Asad
on his arrival found the rebels in possession of all Eastern
Khurāsān, and Merv threatened both from the East and
from the South. Sending a force under 'Abdur Raḥmān
b. Nu'aym towards Merv Rūdh to keep Hārith's main
body in check, he marched himself against the rebel
forces at Āmul and Zamm. These took refuge in the
citadel of Zamm, and Asad, having thus checked the
insurgents in this quarter, continued his march on Balkh.
Meanwhile Hārith seems to have retreated before ' Abdur-
Raḥmān towards Balkh and thence across the Oxus,
where he laid siege to Tirmidh. Lower Tukhāristān
returned to its allegiance ; on the other hand Hārith
was now supported not only by the kings of Khuttal
and Nasaf, but also, as appears from later events, by
the Jabghu of Tukhāristān. The government troops were
unable to cross the Oxus in the face of Hārith's army ;
finding, however, that the garrison was well able to defend
itself, they returned to Balkh, while Hārith, after falling
out with the king of Khuttal, seems to have retired into

*T*ukhāristān. Here, following the example of Mūsā b. Khāzim at Tirmidh, he made a safe retreat for himself in Badakhshān.

The motives of *H*ārith's rebellion have been most variously estimated. In spite of the unctuous sentiments which he is represented as uttering on all occasions, it is hard to find in him the " pious Muslim, ascetic and reformer " whom van Vloten too sharply contrasts with the government officials (**17**). In spite too of the prominent position given to him in the Arabic chronicles, it may even be questioned whether he and his small personal following were not rather the tools than the leaders of the elements making for the overthrow of the Umayyad administration in Khurāsān. At all events the weakness of his hold over his temporary followers is much more striking than his transient success. Further evidence of this is given in a most important narrative prefaced by *T*abarī to his account of Asad's expedition into *S*ughd. Except for the scantiest notices, the Arabic historians have nothing to say regarding the effects of the war in Khurāsān on the situation in Transoxania. Wellhausen's conclusion (based apparently on *T*abarī 1890. 6) that " *H*ārith first unfurled the black flag in Transoxania in the last year of Junayd " is scarcely tenable. There is further no evidence at all for his assumption that Samarqand had fallen into the hands of the *H*ārithites, especially as Bukhārā remained loyal to the administration. That Asad's expedition was not, in fact, directed against *H*ārith follows in the clearest possible manner from the narrative referred to (*T*ab. 1585. 6–16).

" Then Asad marched towards Samarqand by way of Zamm, and when he reached Zamm, he sent to Al-Haytham ash-Shaybānī, one of Hārith's followers, who was in Bādhkar (the citadel of Zamm), saying " That which you have disowned in your own people is only their evil ways, but that does not extend to the women . . . *nor to the conquest by the unbelievers of such as Samarqand*. Now I am on my way to Samarqand and I take an oath before God that no harm shall befall you on my initiative, but you shall have friendly and honourable treatment and pardon, you and those with you. . . ."

So Al-Haytham came out to join him on the condition of pardon
which he had given him, and Asad pardoned him, and Al-Haytham
marched with him to Samarqand and Asad gave them double pay."

The expedition therefore was obviously against unbelievers. That the whole of Sughd was lost to the Arabs
is clear from the fact that Asad found it necessary to take
provisions for the army with him from Bukhārā. He was
not successful in recapturing the city, however, and
attempted no more than the damming of the canal
sluices at Waraghsar.

The fate of the garrison of Samarqand has thus been
passed over in silence, unless, perhaps, it is hinted at in
Asad's reference to the capture of Muslim women.
Whether Ghūrak recaptured it with his own troops or
with the aid of the Türgesh, it can scarcely be doubted
that he had taken advantage of the dissensions in
Khurāsān to realise his ambition and at last drive the
Arabs out of his capital. Of all the conquests of Qutayba
beyond the Oxus, Bukhārā, Chāghaniān, and perhaps
Kish alone remained to the Arabs. A confirmatory
detail is the cessation of Sughdian embassies to China
between 731 and 740 : now that independence (even if
under Türgesh suzerainty) had been won again, there was
no need to invoke Chinese support. Negative evidence
of the same kind is afforded by the absence of any Arab
embassy during the same period. Had the Arabs been in
possession of Sughd, it is practically certain that Asad,
as he had done before, would have renewed relations with
the Chinese court. Against this view may be set the
statement in *T*ab. 1613. 5 that Khāqān was preparing an
army to invest Samarqand at the time of his assassination. This report is, however, from its nature untrust-
worthy, and is contradicted by the presence of the king
of Sughd with Sughdian troops in the Türgesh army in
119/737 as well as by Naṣr b. Sayyār's expedition to
Samarqand two years later. Sughd thus enjoyed once
more a brief period of independence. In 737 or 738
Ghūrak died and his kingdom was divided amongst his

heirs.   He was succeeded at Samarqand by his son Tu-ho
(? Tarkhūn), formerly prince of Kabudhān.   Another
son Me-chu'o (? Mukhtār) was already king of Māyamurgh,
while the king of Ishtīkhan in 742 was a certain Ko-lo-
pu-lo who may perhaps be identified with Ghūrak's
brother Afarūn (18).

The year after the campaigns against Hārith, 118/736,
was devoted by Asad to the reorganisation of his province,
including a measure which, it seems, he had already
projected in his first term of office.   This was the
removal of the provincial capital from Merv to Balkh
(19).   Since no other governor of Khurāsān followed
his example we must seek the motive for the innovation
either in the contemporary situation in Khurāsān
and Transoxania or in Asad's personal views.   Explanations based on the former are not hard to find.   Asad,
on taking office, had been faced with a serious situation
both in Lower Tukhāristān and across the river.   He
had obviously to establish a strong point d'appui.   The
loyalty of the garrison at Merv was not above suspicion
but the garrison at Balkh was composed of Syrian troops,
who could be trusted to the uttermost (20).   Merv was
also less convenient for reaching Tukhāristān, which was
at the moment the main area of operations.   More
important still, perhaps, Balkh was the centre from which
all disturbances spread in Eastern Khurāsān, as in the
revolt of Nēzak and the recent attempt of Hārith.   As
the holding of Balkh had enabled Qutayba to forestall
Nēzak, it is possible that Asad felt that in Balkh he would
be in a position to check all similar movements at the
beginning.   Other considerations may also have disposed
him to take this view.   Balkh was the traditional capital
and on it, as we have seen, was focussed the local sentiment of Eastern Khurāsān.   Merv, on the other hand,
had always been the capital of the foreigners, of the
Sāsānians before the Arabs.   Asad's personal friendship
with the dihqāns may have given him some insight into
the moral effect which would follow from the transference

of the adminsitration to the centre of the national life. Still greater would this effect be when the rebuilding was carried out not by the Arabs themselves but by their own people under the supervision of the Barmak, the hereditary priest-ruler of the ancient shrine. Quite apart from this, however, the rebuilding of Balkh was an event of the greatest significance, and once restored it soon equalled, if it did not eclipse, its rival Merv in size and importance. While the new city was being built, the army was employed in expeditions into Tukhāristān, for the most part under the command of Juday' al-Karmānī, who achieved some successes against the followers of Hārith and even succeeded in capturing their fortress in Badakshhān. Other raids were undertaken by the governor himself, but without results of military importance.

Asad now planned a more ambitous expedition against Khuttal, partly in retaliation for the assistance given to Hārith, partly, it may be, to wipe off an old score. The chronology presents some difficulties at this point. Tabarī relates two expeditions into Khuttal in the same year 119/737, both from the same source, but that which is undoubtedly the earlier is dated towards the close of the year (Ramadān = September). Wellhausen avoids the difficulty by referring this expedition to 118, reckoning back from the appointment of Nasr b. Sayyār, the data for which are full and unimpeachable. This would seem the obvious solution were it not that the date given in the Chinese records for the assassination of Su-Lu, 738 (**21**), agrees perfectly with Tabarī's dating of the Battle of Kharīstān in Dec. 737. The presence of Asad on the second expedition would then hang together with the "somewhat legendary" narrative of the Mihrjān feast. There seems reason, therefore, for dating this expedition in 120/738 and regarding it as having been despatched by Asad, though not actually accompanied by him. Tabarī fortunately preserves also a short notice of the situation in Khuttal. The heir of as-Sabal,

G

whose name is to be read as Al-Hanash, from the Chinese transcription Lo-kin-tsie (22), had fled to China, possibly on account of factional disturbances.   On his deathbed as-Sabal appointed a regent, Ibn As-Sā'ijī, to govern the country until Al-Hanash could be restored.   The moment was certainly opportune for making an expedition and Asad at first carried all before him.   On his first appearance, however, Ibn As-Sā'ijī had appealed for aid to Su-Lu, who was at his capital Nawākath (on the Chu).   The Khāqān, with a small mounted force including the Sughdian refugees, marched from Sūyāb (near Tokmak, on the Chu) to Khuttal in seventeen days, only to find Asad, warned of his approach by the regent, who was endeavouring to play both sides off against each other, in precipitate retreat.   The baggage train had been despatched in advance under Ibrāhīm b. 'Āsim with a guard of Arabs and native troops from Chaghānian but the main body was overtaken by the Turks as it was crossing the river and suffered severe losses.   Asad, considering himself safe with the river between his army and the enemy, encamped and sent orders to Ibrāhīm to halt and entrench his position.   The Turks, however, were able to effect a crossing ; after an unsuccessful assault on Asad's camp, they hastened to overtake the richer prize while the governor's troops were too worn out to protect it.   By sending a party under cover to fall on the troops of Chaghānian from the rear while he himself attacked in front, the Khāqān forced an entrance into Ibrāhīm's camp.   Chāghān Khudāh, faithful to the last, himself fell with the greater part of his forces but the remainder of the garrison were saved by the timely arrival of Asad.   According to the main account, the Arabs were allowed to withdraw to Balkh without further serious fighting.   A variant account given by Tabarī relates an unsuccessful assault by the Türgesh on Asad's camp on the morning following the " Battle of the Baggage," which happened to be the feast of Fitr (1st October 737).   On the retiral of the Arabs, the

Khāqān, instead of returning to his capital with the honours of the day, remained in Tukhāristān.

Here he was joined by Hārith, who advised him to undertake a winter raid into Lower Tukhāristān while the Arab troops were disbanded, undoubtedly in the expectation that the local princes would again unite with him against Asad. The governor retained his army at Balkh until the winter had set in, and in the meantime the Khāqān summoned forces to join him from Sughd and the territories subject to Tukhāristān. The enumeration which Tabarī gives of the troops accompanying the Khāqān on this expedition shows very clearly how completely Arab rule in Transoxania and the Oxus basin had been supplanted by that of the Turks. We are told that besides the Khāqān's own Turkish troops and Hārith with his followers there were present the Jabghu, the king of Sughd, the prince of Usrūshana, and the rulers of Shāsh and Khuttal. It is fairly certain, of course, that the list is exaggerated in so far as the actual presence of the princes is concerned (it is in fact partially contradicted in other parts of the narrative), but it can scarcely be doubted that forces from some, if not all, of these principalities were engaged. On the evening of the 9th Dhu'l-Hijja (7th Dec.) news reached Balkh that the Türgesh with their auxiliaries, numbering some 30,000, were at Jazza. Asad ordered signal fires to be lit and with the Syrian garrison of Balkh and what other troops he could muster from the district marched out against them. The governor of Khulm sent in a second report that the Khāqān, having been repulsed in an attack on the town, had marched on towards Pērōz Nakhshēr, in the neighbourhood of Balkh. From this point the enemy, avoiding Balkh, moved on Jūzjān and occupied the capital (23). Instead of continuing his advance immediately, the Khāqān halted here and sent out raiding parties of cavalry in all directions, an action which put it beyond doubt that the immediate object of the expedition was not the capture of Merv but the rousing of Lower

Tukhāristān against the Arabs. Contrary to Hārith's expectations, however, the king of Jūzjān joined with the Arabs, who marched towards Shubūrqān by way of Sidra and Kharīstān. From the conflicting narratives in Tabarī, it seems that Asad surprised the Khāqān in the neighbourhood of Kharīstān (or Sān) at a moment when his available forces amounted only to 4,000. A furious struggle ensued, which was decided in favour of the Arabs by an assault on the Khāqān from the rear, on the initiative of the king of Jūzjān. It is in connection with the battle, which he describes as if it were a set engagement in which the whole of the opposing forces were engaged, that Tabarī gives his list of the combatants. But as only 4,000 out of the total of 30,000 troops with the Khāqān were involved, the list is obviously out of place and the whole narrative shows the marks of rehandling. The Muslims gained an overwhelming success : the Khāqān and Hārith, having narrowly escaped capture in the confusion, were closely followed by Asad as far as Jazza, when a storm of rain and snow prevented further pursuit. They were thus able to regain the Jabghu in Tukhāristān, with happier fortune than the raiding parties, whose retreat was cut off by the vigilance of Al-Karmānī, and of whom only a single band of Sughdians made good their escape.

On this skirmish at Kharīstān, for it was little more, hung the fate of Arab rule, not only in Transoxania, but possibly even in Khurāsān, at least for the immediate future. Though the princes of Lower Tukhāristān fought for Asad in the first place, there can be little doubt that a victory for Su-Lu would have swung them back to the side of Hārith and the Turks, who would then have been in a position to follow up their attacks with the advantage of a base at Balkh, solidly supported by the Oxus provinces. From such a danger the Arabs were saved only by Asad's resolution and fortunate selection of Balkh as his residence. The account given of Hishām's incredulity on hearing the report shows how very serious

the outlook had been and the extent to which the name of
the Khāqān had become an omen of disaster. Kharīstān
was not only the turning point in the fortunes of the Arabs
in Central Asia, but gave the signal for the downfall of
the Türgesh power, which was bound up with the personal
prestige of Su-Lu. The princes of Tukhāristān and
Transoxania found it expedient to treat him with respect
as he was returning to Nawākath, but in his own country
the dissensions long fomented in secret by the Chinese
broke out. Su-Lu was assassinated by the Baga Tarkhan (Kūrsūl) ; the kingdom fell to pieces. " the Turks
split up and began to raid one another," and the *coup de
grâce* of the Khanate was delivered at Sūyāb in 739 by
the faction of Kūrsūl, supported by the Chinese and
with the assistance of Al-Ishkand and contingents from
Shāsh and Farghāna (24) (25). With the collapse of the
Türgesh kindgom disappeared the last great Turkish
confederation in Western Asia for more than two
centuries to come. The battle of Kharīstān assured
the supremacy of the Muslim civilisation in Sogdiana, but
it could not have attained the richness of its full development there unless all danger from the steppes had been
removed. That this security was attained was due not
to the Arabs, but to the Chinese diplomacy, which, by
breaking down the greatest external obstacle to the
Muhammadan penetration of Central Asia, brought itself
face to face with the Arabs. This could scarcely have
been realised at once, however, by the Arab government,
whose immediate task was to restore its lost authority
in Transoxania.

NOTES

1. As the history of this and the following period has been given in considerable
detail by Wellhausen (Arab. Reich 280 ff.) from the Arab point of view, it is
intended in these chapters to follow only the situation in Transoxania
and the course of the Türgesh conquests, avoiding as far as possible a
simple recapitulation of familiar matter. Thus little reference is made to
the factional strife among the Arabs, though it naturally played a very
important part in limiting their power to deal with the insurgents.
2. See Chavannes, Documents 285, n. 3.

3.   *Cf.* Tab. II. 1718. 3 ff.
4.   Tab. 1462. 11 ; *cf.* 1688. 10, 1481 f.
5.   Tab. 1690. 16.
6.   Chav. Doc. 206 f., 293 f.
7.   Van Vloten, La Domination Arabe 28.
8.   Tab. 1533. 15.
9.   Tab. 1501. 2.
10. Wellhausen 284 f. : van Vloten 22 f. : Tab. 1507 f. : Bal. 428 f.
11. See Wellhausen 218.
12. The variant readings in Tab. 1509. 11. (*cf.* Ibn al-Athīr) make it doubtful whether the taxes were reimposed on them or not.
13. Tab. 1514. 11.
14. See Yāqūt s.v. : Barthold, Turkestan 127 : and *cf.* Tab. 1523. 3.   The chief difficulty in Tabarī's text is the abrupt change at the last word of l. 14 on p. 1516 : thumma ta*h*awwala (ashrashu) ilā marjin yuqālu lahu bawā-daratun *fa'atāhum* sabābatun . . . wahum nuzūlun bikamarjata.   The context shows that it was not to Ashras that Sabāba came but to the garrison of Kamarja with the news that the Khāqān was retiring past them (mārrun bikum).
15. The chronological difficulties are explained by Wellhausen 285 ff.   They are of small importance however, and it seems preferable to follow his dates for these campaigns.
16. *Cf.* Tab. 1528. 9. with 1529. 5 f. 14 f.
17. Van Vloten, *op. cit.* 29 ff. : Wellhausen 289 ff. (*cf.* 302 f.).   Another account of *H*ārith is given by Gardīzī ap. Barthold Turkestan, Texts pp. 1–2.
18. Chav. Doc. 210, 136, 140 ; Barthold, Arab. Quellen 21. n. 8.
19. Tab. 1490, 1591. 18 : Wellhausen 292 and 284 n. : Barthold in Zeitschrift fur Assyriologie XXVI (1911) 261.
20. Tab. 1590. 5.   There does not seem to be any record of when these Syrians were settled at Balkh.
21. Wieger 1643 : Chav. Doc. 284 f.
22. Chav. Doc. 168.
23. As Jūzjān is distinguished from Shubūrqān in Tāb. 1608. 17, it is probable that this was the town Kundurm or Qurzumān mentioned in Ya'qūbī's Geog. 287.
24. Tab. 1613 : Chav. Doc. 83 f., 122 n.   As regards the adjective Kharlukhī applied to the Jabghu in 1612. 16, the most satisfactory explanation is that given by Marquart, Hist. Glossen 183 f.
25. The frequent references in the Chinese annals to the association of Se-kin-t'i, king of Kish, with the Türgesh raise an interesting problem.   There can be no doubt that he is the same prince as Al-Ishkand, ruler of Nasaf, in the Arabic records.   The name is Iranian and personal, not dynastic. (See Justi's Iranisches Namenbuch).   Al-Ishkand is first mentioned in the account of the Battle of the Pass, (Tab. 1542. 8) where he appears in command of a cavalry force on the side of the Khāqān, though Kish and Nasaf were both in the hands of the Arabs (1545. 1).   The forces which he commanded were therefore not the ordinary local troops.   During *H*ārith's siege of Tirmidh he received reinforcements from Al-Ishkand, but no statement is made on the composition of his forces.   He is

mentioned again as accompanying the Khāqān and the Sughdians in the attack on Asad before the " Battle of the Baggage " (1597. 17–18, where the reading ' Ispahbadh of Nasā ' is probably an error in the tradition. Again there can be no question here of local troops from Nasaf or Kish. In the Chinese records Se-kin-t'i appears as the commander of an independent force, not merely a detachment of Turks or levies from Shāsh or Farghāna. The most reasonable conclusion is that Al-Ishkand was the commander of the corps of Sughdian refugees.   This would explain the title " King of the Warriors " by which he is sometimes mentioned in the Chinese records (Chav. Doc. 147 n. 1 and 313).   The actual term (Chākar) from which the title was derived does not appear in the Arabic histories in this connection, but it is perhaps possible that a variant of the name (derived from *razm*) is to be read in Tab. 1614. 2 for the meaningless " razābin al-Kissī."   In 1609. 15 a force of " Bābīya " is mentioned along with the Sughdians, and the name, though unrecognisable, probably refers to some forces connected with Sughd.   Wellhausen's conclusion that the Sughdians and " Bābīya " formed part of the personal following of Hārith b. Surayj seems to force the connection in the text too far (hamala 'l-hārithu waman ma'ahu min ahli's-sughdi wal-bābīyati).   On the other hand, since al-Ishkand appears as the ally of Hārith, we may conclude that some understanding existed between the latter and the Sughdians (and therefore the Turks) at the time of his revolt.   It is probable that the Sughdian corps assisted in the recovery of Samarqand from the Arabs.

V. THE RECONQUEST OF TRANSOXANIA.

THE reaction produced by the downfall of the Türgesh power was manifested in Transoxania in the first place by an increased regard for China. The princes had found the Türgesh yoke no less galling in the end than that of the Arabs (1) ; the country was as wasted and impoverished by their continual raids as it had been under the latter. The profitable native and transit trade, the source of the entire wealth of the cities, must have shrunk to negligible proportions if it had not wholly ceased. All classes of the people therefore were weary of war and sought only a peace consonant with their self-respect. For the attainment of these aims it was vain to look to China ; the granting of bombastic titles to a few princes brought neither comfort nor aid. A final opportunity was thus offered to wise statesmanship to swing the whole country round to the Arabs almost without a blow. For two years, however, the situation seemed to remain much as it was, except for an expedition into Khuttal, probably on the pretext of assisting the ruling house against a usurper from Bamiyān. Nevertheless some progress had been made by the administration in regaining the prestige it had lost. This was due not merely to the effect of the victories over Hārith and the Türgesh, but even more to Asad's personal relations with the dihqāns. He had, as we have seen, gratified the national pride of the people of Tukhāristān by transferring the seat of power from Merv, the capital of the foreigners, to Balkh, the centre of their national life. As had been the case even in his first term of office, he was able to attract to his side many of the more influential elements in Lower Tukhāristān and the Ephthalite lands—to this, in fact, was largely due his success in the struggle with the Turks. More striking evidence still is afforded by the conversion

of the dihqāns at this period, amongst them the minor
chief Sāmān-Khudāh and probably also the Barmak.
By this means Asad laid the foundations for a true
reconciliation and Narshakhī's work amply attests the
honour which later generations attached to his name.
His work was of course incomplete in that it was practically confined to the ruling classes and naturally did not
extend to the now independent dihqāns of Sughd.

Early in 120/738 Asad died, and after a lapse of some
months the governorship was conferred by Hishām on
Nasr b. Sayyār. For the subject peoples no choice
could have been more opportunely made. Nasr was
one of the few men who had come with honour and
reputation through the external and internal conflicts
of the last thirty years. Belonging to the small and
almost neutral tribe of Kināna, his position bore a strong
similarity to that of Qutayba in that both were more
dependent on the support of a powerful patron than on
their tribal connexions, and therefore, though favouring
Qays, less frantically partisan. In contrast to Qutayba,
however, Nasr, after thirty years of active leadership, knew the situation in Khurāsān, Transoxania,
and Central Asia as no Arab governor had ever done.
He had seen the futility of trying to hold the country
by mere brute force, and the equal futility of trying to
dispense with force. While he held the support of
Hishām, therefore, he set himself to restore Arab authority
in Transoxania. The appointment of Qatan b. Qutayba,
who had inherited much of his father's ability, to
command the forces beyond the river gave earnest
of an aggressive policy. The appointment was not to
Samarqand, as Wellhausen says, but " over Sughd,"
i.e., the garrisons in Bukhārā and probably Kish, who were
responsible in the first place for keeping the surrounding
districts in subjection. The governor himself then carried
out a brief expedition, intended apparently to punish
some rebels in the neighbourhood of the Iron Gate,
possibly in Shūmān. Having thus vindicated the

authority of the administration, Nasr returned to Merv
and delivered the famous Khuṭba in which the system of
taxation and conditions of amnesty were at last laid down
in a form satisfactory to the mawālī and the subject
peoples (2). The results were as he had foreseen. The
princes and people of Transoxania submitted, as far as
we can judge, without opposition when Nasr with his army
marched through Sughd to re-establish the Arab garrison
and administration in Samarqand.

This expedition may in all probability be dated in
121/739. A year or two later, Nasr collected his forces,
which included levies from Transoxania, for an attack
on Shāsh. Wellhausen considers that the first two
expeditions were only stages of the third, but the
expedition to Shāsh can hardly have taken place earlier
than 122/740, in view of the fact that the armies of Shāsh
and Farghāna were engaged with the Türgesh in 739,
and of Narshakhī's statement (3), which there is no reason
to dispute, that Tughshāda was assassinated in the thirty-
second year of his reign. Reckoning in lunar years this
gives 122 (91–122), in solar years 123 (710–741), as the
date. This is confirmed by the Chinese record of an
embassy from Shāsh in 741 complaining that " Now
that the Turks have become subject to China, it is only
the Arabs that are a curse to the Kingdoms " (4). 123 is
also the date given for the return of the Sughdians (5).
It is most unlikely that the intervening year or years
passed without expeditions altogether, and the most
reasonable supposition is that they were occupied in the
pacification of Sughd. The expedition marched east-
ward through Ushrūsana, whose prince, as usual, paid
his allegiance to the victor on his passage, but on reaching
the Jaxartes Nasr found his crossing opposed by the army
of Shāsh, together with Hārith b. Surayj and some
Turkish troops. It would seem that he was unable to
come to blows with the main body of the enemy, but
made a treaty with the king by which the latter agreed
to accept an Arab resident and to expel Hārith, who was

accordingly deported to Fārāb.   As usual, later tradition
magnified the exploits of the Arabs by crediting Nasr
with the capture and execution of Kūrsūl, the Türgesh
leader who had been scarcely less redoubtable than the
Khāqān himself.   If the story has any foundation it is
probably a legendary development from the capture
of a Turkish chief Al-Akhram, related by Tabarī in a
variant account.   The presence of Kūrsūl with a Türgesh
force on this occasion is not in itself impossible, but if his
identification with Baga Tarkhan is sound, we know that
he was executed by the Chinese in 744/126 (6).   The
expulsion of Hārith was probably the object for which the
expedition had been undertaken ;   before returning,
however, the Arabs entered Farghāna and pursued its
king as far as Qubā before bringing him to terms.   The
negotiations were carried out between Sulaymān b.
Sūl, one of the princes of Jūrjān, and the Queen-Mother.
This invasion of Farghāna is related in three (or four)
different versions, some of which may possibly refer to a
second expedition mentioned by Tabarī later.   In the
same year, on returning from the expedition to Shāsh,
Nasr was met at Samarqand by the Bukhār Khudāh
Tughshāda and two of his dihqāns.   The nobles laid a
complaint against the prince, but as Nasr seemed indis-
posed to redress their grievance, they attempted to
assassinate both the Bukhār Khudāh and the Arab
intendant at Bukhārā, Wāsil b. 'Amr.   The former
was mortally wounded, and succeeded by his son Qutayba,
so named in honour of the conqueror.   The incident is
related also by Narshakhi with some additional details
which profess to explain the assassination.   The two
narratives present such a remarkable similarity of phrase,
however, even though they are in different languages,
that it is rather more likely that the Persian version has
elaborated the story than that Tabarī deliberately
suppressed any offensive statements, as argued by van
Vloten (7).

Except for a possible second expedition to Farghāna,

no other campaigns into Transoxania are recorded of
Nasr, unless Balādhurī's tradition (from Abū 'Ubayda)
of an unsuccessful attack on Ushrūsana refers to a
separate expedition. This is unlikely, and the account
conflicts with that given in Tabarī. Ushrūsana, however,
was never really subdued until nearly a century later.
Tukhāristān, if it had not already been recovered by
Asad, may have made submission of its own accord.
Since the defeat of the Türgesh and the flight of Hārith
it had ceased to hold any menace to the Arabs, and Nasr
had accordingly retransferred the capital to Merv on his
appointment.

The governor now turned his attention to restoring
the prosperity of the country and developing a policy
of co-operation with the subject peoples. Nasr was the
first Arab ruler of Transoxania to realise that the government depended for support in the last resort on the
middle classes and agriculturalists. Both these classes
were of greater political importance perhaps in Transoxania, with its centuries of mercantile tradition, than
any other were in the Empire. It was in the same
way that in later years the Tāhirids and Sāmānids
established their ascendancy (8). He was thus able not
only to complete the work begun by Asad b. 'Abdullah,
but to settle it on more stable foundations. Shortly
after his recapture of Samarqand he had sent an embassy
to China. This was followed up in 126/744 by a much
more elaborate embassy, obviously intended to regulate
commercial relations in the most complete manner
possible, in which the Arabs were accompanied by
ambassadors not only from the Sogdian cities and
Tukhāristān, but even from Zābulistān, Shāsh, and the
Türgesh. Two other Arab embassies are also recorded
in 745 and 747. There can be no doubt that it was not
so much the justice of Nasr's rule as his personal influence
and honesty that reconciled the peoples of Transoxania.
Even the Sughdian refugees, stranded after the dissolu-
tion of the Türgesh confederacy, trusted him to honour

the conditions upon which they had agreed to return, and were not deceived although his concessions raised a storm of protest, and the Caliph himself was brought to confirm them only for the sake of restoring peace.

It is not surprising, however, that the princes were dissatisfied with the success which had attended the pacification of Transoxania. The people were " becoming Arabs " too rapidly and their own authority was menaced in consequence. They were still hopeful of regaining their independence, especially when Nasr's position became less secure after the death of Hishām. We hear therefore of sporadic embassies to China, such as that sent from Ishtīkhan in 745 asking for annexation to China "like a little circumscription." That the governor was aware of this undercurrent may be judged from the fact that he felt it necessary to have Hārith b. Surayj pardoned, in case he should again bring in the Turks to attack the government (9). But the people as a whole held for Nasr. The respect and even affection which he inspired held all Transoxania true to him during the last troubled years. No tribute could be more eloquent than the facts that not a single city in Transoxania took advantage of the revolutionary movements in Khurāsān to withdraw its allegiance, that Abū Muslim's missionaries went no further than the Arab colonies at Āmul, Bukhārā, and Khwārizm, and that the loyal garrison of Balkh found first support and then refuge in Chaghāniān and Tukhāristān. On these facts the various authorities whose narratives are related by Tabari completely agree, and by their agreement disprove the exaggerated account given by Dīnawarī (359 f.) that " Abū Muslim sent his envoys (duʻāt) to all quarters of Khurāsān, and the people rallied en masse to Abū Muslim from Herāt, Būshanj, Merv-Rūdh, Tālaqān, Merv, Nasā, Abīward, Tūs, Naysābūr, Sarakhs, Balkh, Chaghāniān, Tukhāristān, Khuttalān, Kish, and Nasaf." Dīnawarī himself states a little later that Samarqand joined Abū Muslim only after the death of Nasr. Abū Muslim's

main strength, in fact, was drawn from Lower Tukhāristān and the neighbourhood of Merv-Rūdh, several of the
princes of which, including the ruler of Būshanj and
Khālid b. Barmak, declared for him.   But even here the
people were not solidly against the administration.
We are told that a camp was established at Jīranj
(south of Merv) " to cut off the reinforcements of Naṣr
b. Sayyār from Merv-Rūdh, Balkh, and the districts of
(Lower) Tukhāristān."   Herāt fell to Abū Muslim
by force of arms.   The Syrian garrison of Balkh, together
with the Muḍarite party, were supported by the rulers
of both Upper and Lower Tukhāristān, and twice recaptured the city from their stronghold at Tirmidh.
An example of Abū Muslim's efforts to gain over the
Iranians is afforded by an incident when, having taken
300 Khwārizmian prisoners in an engagement, he
treated them well and set them free (**10**).

The tradition of the enthusiasm of the Iranians for
Abū Muslim is true only of the period after his success.
In our most authentic records there is no trace of a mass
movement such as has so often been portrayed.   His
following was at first comparatively so small that had the
Arabs been more willing to support Naṣr at the outset,
it is practically certain that it would have melted away as
rapidly as the following of Ḥārith b. Surayj at the first
reverse.   " Nothing succeeds like success," and Abū
Muslim, once victorious on so imposing a scale, and that
with the aid of Iranians, became a heroic figure among
the peoples of Eastern Khurāsān.   The legend penetrated
but slowly into Transoxania.   When by 130/748, however,
the whole of Eastern Khurāsān had fallen to Abū Muslim
and Naṣr no longer held authority, his governors in
Transoxania were replaced by the nominees of Abū
Muslim without outward disturbance.   But the recru-
descence of embassies to China shows that under the
surface currents were stirring.   Shāsh had already
thrown off its allegiance and the Sogdian princes had by
no means lost all hope of regaining independence in

spite of the tranquillity of the last few years. As it happened, however, the first revolt was not on their part but by the Arab garrison of Bukhārā under Sharīk b. Shaykh in 133/750–751. The rising, which was due to their resentment at the seizure of the Caliphate by the 'Abbāsids and the passing over of the 'Alid house, was suppressed with some difficulty by Abū Muslim's lieutenant Ziyād b. Sāli*h* assisted by the Bukhār Khudāh. The fact that the Bukhār-Khudāh assisted the troops of Abū Muslim against Sharīk might be regarded as an indication that he belonged to the party of the former. This inference is more than doubtful, however. Of the 30,000 men, who, we are told, joined the rebels, probably the greater part were the townsmen, or " popular party," of Bukhārā. The revolt thus assumed the domestic character of a movement against the aristocratic party, who, led by the Bukhār-Khudāh, naturally co-operated with the Government in its suppression. The events of the following year are sufficient evidence against any other explanation. According to Narshakhī, who gives by far the fullest account of this revolt, Ziyād had also to suppress a similar movement in Samarqand. In the same year an expedition was sent into Khuttal by Abū Dāwud, the governor of Balkh. Al-*H*anash at first offered no opposition ; later in the campaign he attempted to hold out against the Arabs but was forced to fly to the Turks and thence to China where he was given the title of Jabghu in recompense for his resistance (**11**). By this expedition Khuttal was effectively annexed to the Arab government for the first time.

Of much greater, and indeed decisive, importance were the results of an expedition under Ziyād b. Sāli*h* into the Turkish lands beyond the Jaxartes. It is surprising to find no reference to this either in *T*abarī or any other of the early historians. A short notice is given by Ibn al-Athīr, drawn from some source which is now apparently lost. The earliest reference which we find in the Arabic histories seems to be a passing mention of Ziyād b.

Sāli*h*'s expedition " into Sīn " in a monograph on Baghdād by Ibn Tayfūr (d. 250/983) (12). For a detailed
account of the battle we are therefore dependent on the
Chinese sources (13). In 747 and 749 the Jabghu of
Tukhāristān had appealed to China for aid against
certain petty chiefs who were giving trouble in the Gilghit
and Chitral valleys. The governor of Kucha despatched
on this duty a Corean officer, Kao-hsien-shih, who
punished the offenders in a series of amazing campaigns
over the high passes of the Karakorum. Before returning
to Kucha after the last campaign he was called in by the
King of Farghāna to assist him against the king of
Shāsh. Kao-hsien-shih at first came to terms with the king
of Shāsh but when on some pretext he broke his word and
seized the city, the heir to the kingdom fled to Sughd for
assistance and persuaded Abū Muslim to intervene.
A strong force was accordingly despatched under Ziyād
b. Sāli*h*. The Chinese, with the army of Farghāna and the
Karluks (who had succeeded the Türgesh in the hege-
mony of the Western Turks), gave battle at Athlakh,
near Tarāz, in July 751 (Dhu'l-*h*ijja 133). During the
engagement the Karluks deserted and Kao-hsien-shih,
caught between them and the Arabs, suffered a crushing
defeat. Though this battle marks the end of Chinese
power in the West, it was in consequence of internal
disruption rather than external pressure. Nothing was
further at first from the minds of the princes of Sughd than
the passing of the long tradition of Chinese sovereignty,
indeed it blazed up more strongly than ever. For had
not a Chinese army actually visited Shāsh on their very
borders ; even if the Arabs had won the first battle, would
they not return to avenge the defeat ? For the last
time the Shao-wu princes planned a concerted rising in
Bukhārā, Kish, Sughd, and Ushrūsana. But China gave
neither aid nor encouragement ; the presence of Abū
Muslim at Samarqand overawed the Sughdians, and only
at Kish did the revolt assume serious proportions. Abū
Dāwud's army easily crushed the insurgents in a pitched

battle at Kandak, near Kish, killing the king Al-Ikhrīd and many of the other dihqāns. Amongst the treasures of the royal palace which were sent to Samarqand were " many articles of rare Chinese workmanship, vessels inlaid with gold, saddles, brocades, and other objects d'art." The Bukhār-Khudāh Qutayba and the dihqāns of Sughd also paid for their complicity with their lives (14).

·So ended the last attempt at restoring an independent Sogdiana under the old régime. For some years yet the princes of Sughd, Khwārizm, and Tukhāristān continued to send appeals to China. The Emperor, however, " preoccupied with maintaining peace, praised them all and gave them consolation, then having warned them sent them back to assure tranquillity in the Western lands." Abū Muslim had also, it would seem, realised the importance of maintaining relations with the Chinese court, for a succession of embassies from " the Arabs with black garments " is reported, beginning in the year following the battle of the Talas. As many as three are mentioned in a single year. It is possible that these embassies were in part intended to keep the government informed on the progress of the civil wars in China, though the active interest of the new administration in their commerce would, as before, tend to reconcile the influential mercantile communities to 'Abbāsid rule. The actual deathblow to the tradition of Chinese overlordship in Western Central Asia was given, not by any such isolated incident as the battle of the Talas, but by the participation of Central Asian contingents in the restoration of the Emperor to his capital in 757 (15). Men from the distant lands to whom China had seemed an immeasurably powerful and unconquerable Empire now saw with their own eyes the fatal weaknesses that Chinese diplomacy had so skilfully concealed. From this blow Chinese prestige never recovered.

The complete shattering of the Western Turkish empires by the Chinese policy had also put an end to all

H

possibility of intervention from that side. Transoxania, therefore, was unable to look for outside support, while the reorganization of the Muslim Empire by the early 'Abbāsid Caliphs prevented, not indeed sporadic though sometimes serious risings, but any repetition of the concerted efforts at national independence. The Shao-wu princes and the more important dihqāns continued to exercise a nominal rule until the advent of the Sāmānids, but many of them found that the new policy of the Empire offered them an opportunity of honourable and lucrative service in its behalf and were quick to take advantage of it. On the other hand the frequent revolts in Eastern Khurāsān under the guise of religious movements show that the mass of the people remained unalterably hostile to their conquerors (**16**). In none of these, however, was the whole of Transoxania involved until the rising organized by Rāfi' b. Layth three years after the fall of the Barmakids. The extraordinary success of his movement may partly be ascribed to resentment at their disgrace, but it perhaps counted for something that he was the grandson of Nasr b. Sayyār. Though the revolt failed it led directly to the only solution by which Transoxania could ever become reconciled to inclusion in the Empire of the 'Abbāsids. Whether by wise judgment or happy chance, to Ma'mūn belongs the credit of laying the foundations of the brilliant Muhammadan civilisation which the Iranian peoples of Central Asia were to enjoy under the rule of a dynasty of their own race.

NOTES

1. *Cf.* Tabarī 1594. 14 : 1613. 3 : Chavannes, Documents 142.
2. The details of this measure are discussed by Wellhausen, Das Arabische Reich 297 ff., and van Vloten, Domination Arabe 71 f. Note that Tab. 1689. 5 expressly refers to them as " conditions of peace."
3. Narshakhī 8. 19.
4. Chav., Doc. 142.
5. Tab. 1717 f.
6. Chav., Doc. 286.
7. Van Vloten, *op. cit.* 20. *Cf. e.g.* Tab. 1694.1 with Narsh. 60. 3–5.
8. Barthold, Turkestan 219.

9. *Tab.* 1867.

10. *Tab.* 1956. 17 ; 1966. 10 ; 1997 ff. (this passage is unfortunately defective and has been supplemented by the editor from Ibn al-Athīr) ; 1970. 9. The popularity of Naṣr is demonstrated also by the growth of a tradition round his name. This appears in *Tabarī* somewhat unobtrusively in isolated passages, unfortunately without quotation of Madā'inī's authorities. According to the " Fihrist " (103. 12) Madā'inī wrote two books on the administrations of Asad b. 'Abdullah and Naṣr b. Sayyār, a fact which confirms the special importance of these two governors in the history of Khurāsān. Probably Asad was more popular with the dihqāns and Naṣr with the people.

11. Chav., Doc. 168 : *cf.* Marquart, Ērānshahr 303.

12. Kitāb Baghdād, Band VI ed. H. Keller, p. 8. 12.

13. Chav., Doc. 297 f. ; Wieger, Textes Historiques 1647.

14. *Tab.* III. 79 f. : Narsh. 8 fin. : Chav., Doc. 140, Notes Addit. 86 and 91.

15 Wieger 1684 ff. : Chav., Doc. 158 n. 4 and 298 f. *Cf.* my article " Chinese records of the Arabs in Central Asia " in the Bulletin of the School of Oriental Studies, II. 618 f.

16 A full account of these risings is given by Prof. E. G. Browne in " Literary History of Persia " vol. I, 308 ff.

BIBLIOGRAPHY OF CHIEF WORKS CITED.

A. ORIENTAL AUTHORITIES.

Al-Balādhurī : (1) (*Kitāb al-Ansāb*) *Anonyme Arabische Chronik*, Band XI, ed. W. Ahlwardt, Greifswald, 1883.

——— (2) *Kitāb Futūh al Buldān*, ed. M. J. de Goeje, Leyden, 1865.

Ad-Dīnawarī : *Kitāb al-Akhbār at-Tiwāl*, ed. V. Guirgass, Leyden, 1888, *Fragmenta Historicorum Arabicorum*, vol. I, from Kitāb al-'Uyūn, ed. M. J. de Goeje and P. de Jong, Leyden, 1869.

Ibn al-Athīr : *Ta'rīkh al-Kāmil*, 12 vols., Cairo 1290 A.H.

Ibn Khalliqān, *Biographical Dictionary*, trans. by Baron MacGuckin de Slane, 4 vols., Paris, 1842–1871.

Ibn Khūrdādhbih : *Kitāb al-Masālik wal-Mamālik*, ed. M. J. de Goeje, (Bibl. Geog. Arab. VI), Leyden, 1889.

Ibn Qutayba : *Kitāb al-Ma'ārif*, ed. F. Wüstenfeld, Göttingen, 1850.

Al-Istakhrī : *Kitāb Masālik al-Mamālik*, ed. M. J. de Goeje, (Bibl. Geog. Arab. I), Leyden, 1870.

An-Narshakhī : *Description Topographique et Historique de Boukhara par Mohammed Nerchakhy*, ed. C. Schefer, Paris, 1892.

At-Tabarī : (1) *Annales quos scripsit Abū Ja'far . . . at-Tabarī*, ed. M. J. de Goeje et alii, 15 vols., Leyden, 1879–1901.

——— (2) *Chronique de Tabari traduite sur la version persane de . . . Bel'ami par H. Zotenberg*, 4 vols., Paris, 1867–1874.

Al-Ya'qūbī : (1) *Kitāb al-Buldān*, ed. M. J. de Goeje, (Bibl. Geog. Arab. VII), Leyden, 1892.

——— (2) *Ibn Wadhih qui dicitur Al-Ja'kubi Historiae*, ed. M. Th. Houtsma, 2 vols., Leyden, 1883.

Yāqūt : *Geographisches Worterbuch*, ed. F. Wüstenfeld, 6 vols., Leipzig, 1866–1873.

B. EUROPEAN WORKS.

W. Barthold : (1) *Turkyestan v'Epokhu Mongolskavo Nashyestviya*, St. Petersburg, 1898.

——— (2) *Zur Geschichte des Christenthums in Mittel-Asien vis zur Mongolischen Eroberungen*, German trans. by R. Stübe, Tubingen and Leipzig, 1901.

——— (3) See under Radloff.

——— (4) Articles in *Encyclopaedia of Islam*.

L. Caetani : *Chronographia Islamica*, Paris, 1912—(proceeding).

Léon Cahun : *Introduction a l'Histoire de l'Asie* : *Turcs et Mongols des Origines à* 1450, Paris, 1896.

E. Chavannes : (1) *Documents sur les Tou-Kiue (Turcs) Occidenteaux*, St. Petersburg, 1903.

——— (2) *Notes Additionelles sur les Tou-Kiue Occidentaux, T'oung Pao*, vol. V (1904).

H. Cordier : *Histoire Générale de la Chine*, tome I, Paris, 1920.

M. A. Czaplicka : *The Turks of Central Asia*, Oxford U.P., 1918 (contains a very full bibliography).

Encyclopaedia Britannica, Eleventh Edition, 1910–1911.

Encyclopaedia of Islām, Leyden and London, 1913—(proceeding).

O. Franke : *Beiträge aus Chinesischen Quellen zur Kenntnis der Türkvölker und Skythen Zentralasiens*, Berlin, 1904.

I. Goldziher : *Muhammandanische Studien*, band I, Halle, 1888.

A. von Kremer : *Culturgeschichte des Orients unter den Chalifen*, 2 vols., Vienna, 1875–1877.

G. Le Strange : *The Lands of the Eastern Caliphate*, Cambridge, 1905.

J. Marquart : (1) *Die Chronologie der Alttürkischen Inschriften*, Leipzig, 1898.

——— (2) *Historische Glossen zu den Alttürkischen Inschriften*, W.Z.K.M., vol. XII (1898) pp. 157–200.

——— (3) *Erānshahr* . . ., Berlin, 1901, with notices by :—

W. Bang, in Keleti Szemle III (1902).

E. Chavannes in J.A. Ser. IX t. XVIII (1901).

M. J. de Goeje, in W.Z.K.M. XVI (1902).

Th. Nöldeke, in Z.D.M.G. LVI (1902).

Sir W. Muir : *The Caliphate, its Rise, Decline, and Fall* : New edition, ed. T. H. Weir, Edinburgh, 1915.

Th. Nöldeke : *Geschichte der Perser und Araber zur Zeit der Sasaniden* . . ., Leyden, 1879.

Pauly's Real-Encyclopädie der Classischen Altertumswissenschaft, Neue Bearbeitung, Stuttgart, 1895—(proceeding).

T. Peisker : " The Asiatic Background," *Cambridge Mediaeval History*, vol. I (1911).

W. Radloff : (1) *Die Alttürkischen Inschriften der Mongolei, Neue Folge*, St. Petersburg, 1897 : with appendix by—

W. Barthold : *Die Historische Bedeutung der Alttürk. Inschr.*

—— (2) *Die Alttürkischen Inschriften der Mongolei, Zweite Folge*, St. Petersburg, 1899 : with appendices by—
　　W. Barthold : *Die Alttürk. Insch. und die Arabischen Quellen.*
　　Fr. Hirth : *Nachworte zur Inschrift des Tonjukuk.*

E. Sachau : *Zur Geschichte und Chronologie von Khwārizm*, 2 parts, Vienna, 1873 (S.B.W.A.).

K. Shiratori : *Uber den Wu-sun-stamm in Centralasien, Keleti Szemle* III (1902), pp. 103–140.

F. H. Skrine and E. D. Ross : *The Heart of Asia* : A History of Russian Turkestan, etc., from the Earliest Times. London, 1899.

M. A. Stein : (1) *Ancient Khotan*, Oxford, 1907.

—— (2) *Serindia*, vol. I, Oxford, 1921.

E. Thomas : *Contributions to the Numismatic History of the Early Mohammedan Arabs in Persia*, J.R.A.S. First Series, vol. XII (1850), pp. 253–347.

W. Tomaschek : *Centralasiatische Studien* : I. *Soghdiana*, Vienna, 1877 (S.B.W.A.).

A. Vámbéry : *History of Bokhara from the Earliest Period down to the Present*, London, 1873.

G. van Vloten : *Recherches sur la Domination Arabe, etc., sous le Khali-fat des Omayades*, Amsterdam, 1894.

J. Wellhausen : *Das Arabische Reich und Sein Sturz*, Berlin, 1902.

L. Wieger, S.J. : *Tomes Historiques*, ? 1903–1905

Yüan Chwang : *On Yüan Chwang's travels in India*, T. Watters, 2 vols., London, 1904 (Oriental Translation Fund, New Series, vols. XIV and XV).